30/23   Soc Sci (Gender)
£3.50
J.M

D0277248

A
PLEA FOR WOMAN

A

PLEA FOR WOMAN

BY MARION REID

"Can man be free, if woman be a slave?"

POLYGON
Edinburgh

A Plea For Woman first published in 1843 by William Tait, Edinburgh
2nd edition published in 1845
3rd edition published in London, 1850
First published in U.S.A. in 1845
Reprinted under the title *Woman, her Education and Influence*,
1847. 1848, 1851, 1852
First edition reprinted in 1988 by Polygon,
48 Pleasance, Edinburgh EH8 9TJ

Typeset by EUSPB, 48 Pleasance, Edinburgh EH8 9TJ

Printed and bound by Bell & Bain Ltd., Glasgow

British Library Cataloguing in Publication Data
Reid, Marion
  A plea for woman
  1. Great Britain. Society. Role of women, 1800-1840.
  I. Title
  305.4'2'0941

ISBN 0 948275 56 1

FOREWORD

A Plea For Woman is a landmark book as the first to be written by a woman, for women, specifically arguing that possession of the vote is crucial in ending discrimination against their gender in education and employment, showing that women's condition can improve only when they have a voice in choosing those who make laws.

The question of civil rights for women arose during the French Revolution and it played a part in the Owenite co-operative community in Scotland before surfacing again with the Chartists as they claimed universal suffrage for men. Marion Reid had researched the subject and had evidently read all she could before writing her own book. She herself said that her ideas "may not be positively new", aware that she was taking part in a long campaign to effect a revolution by persuasion, a complete change in the social and legal treatment of the female race.

Something of a best-seller in its day, the book was read by women on both sides of the Atlantic. First published in Edinburgh at 3s. 6d. in 1843, with simultaneous distribution in London and Dublin, it went into a second edition in 1845. A cheap edition was produced by the London distributor at 1s. 6d. in 1850. But interest in America was even greater.

The book first appeared there in 1845. It was reprinted in 1847, 1848, 1851 and 1852 by a different firm under a new title, *Woman, her Education and Influence*. In a foreword to the 1847 edition, the publisher claims that the author has "an enviable reputation" and that the work has been translated into the major European languages. So far, I have been unable to verify the latter statement. It may be publishers' puff or it may not, considering how cheap nineteenth-century books can disintegrate and vanish. What is certain is that many American women read the *Plea* in the years when the American suffrage movement began. This fact is nowhere mentioned in the *History of Woman Suffrage* , a massively detailed and apparently authoritative source which has nevertheless managed to mislead at least one contemporary writer on the influence at work in the first women's rights convention held in 1848 at Seneca Falls.

In her book on Margaret Fuller, Marie Urbanski claims that Seneca Falls was based on *Woman in the Nineteenth Century*, published in

America in 1845 and not reprinted there for ten years, and states that the convention resolutions were inspired by Fuller's book. Had the *History of Woman Suffrage* not hidden American editions of the *Plea* from history, she might have concluded by reading it that the constraints of patriarchy are much the same for women in all industrialised societies, and so are women's criticisms of it. Many of the resolutions at Seneca Falls could have emerged straight from the experience of the women present.

Fuller's book did not call for women to campaign for suffrage, and could not have influenced the ninth resolution, which did. Elizabeth Cady Stanton had to fight hard to get this resolution passed. She fought, says the *History of Woman Suffrage*, "seeing that the power to choose rulers and make laws, was the right by which all others could be secured". This is the fundamental argument of *A Plea For Woman*. The *History of Woman Suffrage* mentions neither Fuller nor Reid as an influence on Seneca Falls, but it is clear from a comparison of editions that many more women were reading Reid than Fuller when the American suffrage movement began to organise. After 1852 the book had outlived its usefulness in America as the movement was then becoming well established.

The *Plea*'s influence is harder to trace in Britain. Christian Johnstone gave it an approving review in 1844, but she thought that a change in attitude resulting in women being trained to keep themselves instead of being obliged to depend on husbands for subsistence would do more for women than formal equality in civil rights. Caroline Ashurst Biggs mentions the book later in the British chapter of the *History of Woman Suffrage* as claiming that civil rights were not incompatible with domestic duties, the point which seems to have struck her most. "Woman's sphere", a mythical zone divorced from parliament and market-place and inhabited by middle-class women, was a great bogey of the times, and the phrase with which Marion Reid exploded the "sphere" was well remembered. A formidable debater, she showed that male opinions as to the nature and extent of the "sphere" differed, and that while they did, it was "not very philosophical" to use the term as if it bore an undisputed meaning. "Not very philosophical" was repeated by Caroline Kirkland in her introduction to American editions of the *Plea*, and it was italicised without attribution by Elizabeth Cady Stanton in her autobiography in 1898: fifty years later, she expected her readers to recognise it. Intelligent women debarred from serious education must have felt a certain glee at seeing a woman take on the arguments of the gender who claimed a monopoly on logical thought, and win.

Students of nineteenth-century history, culture and social theory may be surprised to find Marion Reid anticipating many points made by Harriet Taylor Mill in *Enfranchisement of Women* and John Stuart Mill in *The Subjection of Women*, and I shall not deprive them of the pleasures of discovery. I wish only to point out that while Harriet Mill follows Christian Johnstone in claiming that earning a living is essential to a woman's dignity, John Mill appears emotionally committed to traditional family life. On this point, I feel that Marion Reid may have been more of an influence on John Mill than on Harriet Mill. While she complains that those women who are compelled to work are relegated to the worst jobs and wants them to have a real opportunity to earn an independent living, she thinks "the best and noblest of women" will in fact prefer domesticity. Her vision of men and women co-operating in the advancement of society in sincerity and freedom without changing the traditional structure of the household, or the division of labour by gender, is close to John Mill's.

However, parts of the *Plea* seem startlingly modern. Marion Reid seems fully aware of the psychological effects on women of the male "system of depression" and how constant denigration can produce in them "an inert and subdued state of mind" or laziness and servility. She is angry at the sacrifice of young women's education and development to those of their brothers, and also at the accompanying verbal imperialism which calls a girl leaving school "finished"; "in that phrase one of the evil influences which pervade the education of girls may be seen". We are only now making real efforts to remove these influences in the classroom, and beginning to realise that, as Marion Reid said, the effects on men of an artificially inflated sense of their prerogatives are just as unfortunate as those of constant depreciation on women.

In its time, the *Plea* was less of a theoretical work than an enabling book for women. All the objections to women's rights then current were stated and counter-arguments presented which I have no doubt women began to use. Media influence was not neglected: a typical article is chosen and deconstructed in Chapter VIII, to show how little substance lay in propaganda against civil equality and how easily similar assertions could be resisted. As belief in the Bible was a part of most people's lives, Marion Reid's demonstration that the pursuit of civil equality was compatible with Christianity would have been found valuable and satisfying in its day, freeing women from the fear of accusations of irreligion.

As yet, little is known about the author of the *Plea*. Eldest daughter of a Glasgow merchant, Marion Kirkland married Hugo Reid in 1839 and went to live in Edinburgh. Family and friends discussed the latest ideas about education, society and politics. She was present at the international anti-slavery convention in London in 1840, where she met many women critical of patriarchy, and was shocked at the exclusion of American women speakers from the platform. In her preface, she says that the immediate cause of her decision to write her book was the scornful sneering in place of reasoned argument in popular books on the condition of women, when they pretended to deal with women's aspirations to equal treatment.

Her life held much travel and probably some vicissitudes of fortune. She survived her husband when he died in London in 1872, but seems unknown to the suffrage movement of that time; she had no interest in claiming credit for her contribution. Now, for the first time in a century and a half, this reprint gives easy access to the work of one of the most readable and keenest-minded writers of the early stages of the women's movement.

PREFACE

The following little volume adds another to that not very numerous class of publications which attempt to throw some light on the peculiarities of woman's position in society. It is designed to show, that social equality with man is necessary for the free growth and development of woman's nature; that it could not elevate her to complete equality with man, if she be really inferior to him in physical strength and mental vigour; that there is no good ground for the assumption that the possession and exercise of political privileges are incompatible with the right performance of the home duties of the sex; that this equality belongs of right to woman, as possessed of the same rational and responsible nature as man; and that it would be of benefit also to man, by ennobling the influence over him of that being who is the natural companion of his life.

I am aware that this is by no means the first time that similar opinions have been given to the world; but the expression of them has given rise to many vague and groundless prejudices, to attempt to dispel which has been more immediately my object.

Although this little book is the production of a woman, yet let not the reader believe that *esprit de corps* has had anything to do with the writing of it. I can assure him most truly, that an enthusiastic belief that this is a question of general philanthropy has been my principal inducement.

I will not, however, deny, that the immediately-exciting cause of my setting to write was the scornful sneers—the more scornful in exact proportion to the want of anything like a reasonable argument—of those who write the popular books about woman, when they condescend to notice such opinions as mine. These suggested to me that I ought to do what I could to show that such opinions have some arguments in their favour which are surely weighty enough to save them from utter contempt; and to demand for them, at least, so much attention as is necessary for their refutation.

I have endeavoured to show that the subject is one of vast importance; that such opinions, having been fairly started, must be met—if they can be met effectually—not by laughs and sneers, but by rational argument. I shall willingly acknowledge myself in the wrong, if any one will take the trouble to convince me that I am so; and if reason fails, a little sarcasm will be easily borne: for ridicule is but a feeble antagonist to truth, however powerful it may be as an auxiliary.

I am not without hopes that these pages may be the humble means of bringing forward more able pens on the same subject. The throwing up of a feather shows how the wind blows: therefore, I throw up this feather with pleasure, hoping that many more will follow to give the same indication. Continual dropping weareth away the solid rock: I therefore willingly contribute this drop, in the earnest hope that it may call down many more—so many, that at last they may wear a passage through the hard rock of the customs and prejudices of ages.

LIVERPOOL, *Oct.* 1843.

CONTENTS

CHAPTER I.

INTRODUCTORY.

"Of two modes of treatment, which may be the more proper one—on the one hand, the mode here exemplified, or on the other, a *horse*-laugh, a sneer, an expression of scorn, or a commonplace witticism, the reader will determine." — *Jeremy Bentham.*

> "Such dupes are men to custom, and so prone
> To reverence what is ancient, and can plead
> A course of long observance for its use,
> That even servitude, the worst of ills,
> Because delivered down from sire to son,
> Is kept and guarded as a sacred thing."
> *Cowper.*

In the present age, when precedent and ancient custom are no longer regarded with that blind reverence which has so long retarded, though it was able only to retard, the onward progress of knowledge, happiness, and virtue,—when the meaning of the saying, "Try all things; hold fast that which is good," is beginning to dawn on the minds of men, and the maxim in some degree to be acted upon,—when it is acknowledged that many of the institutions of society are defective, and many others oppressive and tyrannical in their exactions,—when these things are considered, it becomes the duty of every one who doubts the wisdom or justice of those social arrangements which have so long been regarded as a sacred bequest from our forefathers, to give expression to his disapprobation and dissent, in order that the evils, so soon as seen, may be discussed, and, if possible, remedied. And even although the ideas brought forward may not be positively new, still, the reiterated repetition of the same ideas, as they arise and develop themselves in different minds, serves to call attention to the subject, and bring it under frequent discussion, which is the most likely method of arriving at the truth. Entertaining such an opinion, we make no apology for throwing together some thoughts, which have arisen in our mind from time to time, on the social position of woman.

It is now high time—and we are glad to see that many efforts are being made—to call the attention of society, especially of woman herself, to the degraded rank which she holds among the human race. It is well known that, among savage nations, she is the menial slave of her lord; in barbarous states, she is alternately his slave and his plaything; while in lands like our own, which have made considerable progress in civilisation, though she has won for herself many privileges, she is still very far from being allowed legal and social equality. Thus we see that the subjugation of the sex is general and undoubted. This state of things prevails in a greater or less degree in every country, and in every state of society.

Although grateful to acknowledge that in this country her condition is inexpressibly happier than it is among those savage nations, where she is made the hewer of wood and drawer of water to her lordly master; yet we cannot shut our eyes to the fact, that even in this country, her condition, though positively improved, is not much, if at all, improved in relation to that of her lord. Even here she is still kept behind—still regarded too much as a mere appendage of man. She advances, it is true, when he advances; but it is no less true that she is always kept some steps behind him, and that not by any necessity of her nature, but by barriers which he erects to interrupt her progress.

Now, I would fain learn the reason why both sexes are not allowed to advance side by side? Is woman really unworthy of social equality with man? Let the question be thoroughly investigated. Do not allow that you are so, oh! my countrywomen, merely because you have long been considered so.

There has lately been a good deal of discussion on this subject; and we incline to think there is room for much more. That there is the greatest propriety in thoroughly sifting the matter, no one will doubt who has taken note of the influence which the condition of woman— putting her own individual benefit at present out of the question — exerts, in its turn, on that of man. Any person of common observation will at once allow that, in the whole range of the middle and lower classes, the mother is the parent who has most opportunity of influencing the moral education of a family. It is allowed, also, that the impressions made on the heart and understanding in childhood and youth are so much more lasting and vivid than those of maturer years, that they are rarely, if ever, entirely effaced in after-life. Indeed, the power which the mother of a family exerts—either for good or for evil, is beyond calculation. Let her send into the world one child who, through her judicious care, has been filled with the active and enthusiastic love of goodness; with the spirit, to say all at once, of pure and enlightened Christianity; and who can estimate, in its far-reaching and wide-spreading results, the extent of the influence which, through this one child, she may exercise over the generations of men. But the reverse will also hold good. Let her send a child into the world whose temper she has neglected, or perhaps even inflamed by her own evil example, whose principles are altogether unfixed, who has nothing to guide him in the path of duty, much less anything to keep him steadily going forward in it, in spite of strong temptation and great obstacles. The evil influence exercised in this case is as great as the good in the former one. To neither of them is it possible to set any bounds, or to say decidedly, here it must stop short.

What, then, are we to think of the wisdom of the parties who would keep behind in the march of improvement, those in whom is placed so great, so noble a trust,—who do not, on the contrary, afford them every facility for cultivating and strengthening the mind. Yet it is not very long ago since the local government of one of the chief cities of the empire, displayed openly that spirit of sneering and ridicule at the mention of this subject, which we are afraid is but too common in all ranks of society. The councillors, to whom we allude, had some measure proposed to them for providing more effectually the means of education for girls of the middle class of society. In the discussion which followed, none of them pressed the proposed measure; while several of them gave utterance to the sentiment, that these girls would be much better employed learning to make pies and puddings! The matter came to no satisfactory conclusion; and this was the ostensible ground on which it was allowed to drop.

We think it will be generally allowed, that the most favourable circumstance in the education of any youth, is the having a mother of a judicious, sensible, and cultivated mind. And since, in most cases, there is no one individual who exercises such influence over the mind of a child as its mother, is it not true wisdom to provide, as effectively as possible, for this influence being of a healthful and beneficial nature? But will this be done by regarding with indifference, or a most absurd mixture of disdain and jealousy, the efforts of woman herself and her friends, or rather the true friends of the whole race, to raise herself in the scale of being by a more just and liberal education, and by so elevating her position, as to inspire her with a just self-respect, thereby giving her a more proper appreciation of the importance of her duties, and greater authority and influence in performing them? There is a great deal said of Institutions for the training of teachers of youth—and the more accomplished they are of course the better; but there is another class:

3

we speak of mothers, the proper training of whom would do more for education, in the most extensive sense of the word, than any normal school could possibly effect. In this case, the reaction is so obvious and immediate, that the wisdom which would always keep woman behind, seems to us very short-sighted indeed.

Not that we would, by any means, be understood as advocating the enlightenment of woman solely, or even chiefly on that ground,—but we use it as an auxiliary argument, and one of such a tangible nature, as will speak home to men's minds; at the same time protesting, that the true reason for the culture of any human being, is to be found in the benefit which that being derives from cultivation. The improved nature of the influence which the enlightened being exerts upon other minds, is quite a secondary consideration, although it is but too often urged as the only reason for the culture of the female mind. Since, then, the whole human race is interested in this question, we call on man, as well as woman, to examine, with unbiassed judgment, all the arguments which can be produced for the destruction of the system of female depression, instead of attempting to laugh down a question of so much importance. Now that it is fairly roused, we hope it will not be again allowed to slumber till it is finally adjusted.

Before proceeding to the consideration of what we intend to be the principal subject in this little volume—woman's just rights, and the wrongs of which she has to complain—we mean to make a few preliminary observations on "influence", on the use of the phrase "woman's sphere", and the idea which prevails, that woman's sphere is vastly inferior to that of man.

CHAPTER II.

"Action and reaction are equal and contrary."—*Laws of Motion.*

Before entering more deeply into the consideration of the subject, we think it will be profitable to devote a short, but distinct chapter to the examination of some ideas about "influence", which we believe to be very prevalent and not very correct. Our principal object in these remarks will be to point out what we consider to be two great errors; and which we yet find to be, if not plainly expressed, at least continually assumed to be truths, by writers on the condition of woman.

The first is, that her influence is quite sufficient, without any fixed rights or privileges, to obtain for woman even more than justice. The second is, that female influence is the *only* influence—that there is no such thing as male influence.

As to the first of these propositions, we are both willing and happy to believe that the influence of woman procures for her a great deal of tenderness, consideration, and courtesy; but this is true only in individual cases. The personal influence of a woman with her husband, and his kindness and good sense, prevent many a woman from having the least suspicion of the barbarous nature of those laws which would interpose but slight obstacles to her husband's treating her with the most unrelenting tyranny, did this mutual good understanding fail. And the very many instances in which it does completely fail, even in the case of the most deserving women, shows how precarious is the nature of this influence, and how little it is to be depended upon. Although, then, there may be thousands of women whose personal influence has prevented them from ever experiencing any very harsh or unjust treatment,—yet, for the whole *sex*, this so-much-talked-of influence has utterly failed in obtaining even the faintest semblance of justice. We promise to make this sufficiently obvious when we come to examine the nature of the laws in force with regard to woman. We shall then find, that whatever great things influence may do for woman in her private

5

capacity, that it has done comparatively little for the sex in securing them justice when this personal influence fails. And what is the reason of this? Why, the reason is obvious:—man exerts as much—or greater—personal influence as woman does, and has all the privileges of citizenship besides. And this brings us to consider the second error, so often assumed as truth—that female influence is *the* greatest influence.

Very far from this being the truth, we believe that the influence which man exerts over woman is even greater than that of woman over man.

Our principal reason for thinking so, is, that the mind of man—whether essentially so or not—is at present stronger and more vigorous than that of woman; and we believe it to be an established fact, that when two minds of different calibre are brought much into contact, the strong mind will, in nine cases out of ten, obtain the most complete ascendancy over the comparatively-weak mind. It is this consideration which leads us to the conclusion, that the influence exerted by man is, at least, equal to that exerted by woman, if not much superior to it. Yet how often do we see female influence insisted on, while that of man is passed by in total silence. No! influence is not exclusively female; it cannot be exercised by one sex alone upon the other. It seems almost self-evident that it must be reciprocal,—must be exercised by both sexes upon each other,—and most powerfully by the strongest and most privileged. As a proof of this, how often do we see husbands overpowering their wives by this potent instrument alone, and forcing them to submit to injustice, both to themselves and children, from which even our present inefficient laws would protect them, if appealed to.

Let us then hear no more of female influence, as if it were an equivalent for all the rights which man possesses; for the possession of those rights, far from annihilating man's influence, gives it tenfold weight.

The writer of "Woman's Mission" has insisted very much on the conceit—for we can call it nothing else—of giving power to man, and influence to woman. Now, we can see no reason whatever for this division. We think that the theory, that power destroys influence, instead of strengthening and confirming it, is built on a foundation of sand. The partition of power and influence between man and woman certainly does not at present exist,—for man now exercises at least as much influence as woman, and has all his power and privileges to add authority to that influence.

The common sense and justice of the matter seems to us to be—let every one have equality of right or power, and let our own character give us all the influence it can.

The circumstance of any class being deprived of the exercise of political rights, very far from giving that class additional influence, always tends to diminish that which it would naturally exert were its privileges on the same footing as those of others. It will be found that the possession by a man of privileges above his fellow-men, will, at the same time, increase his influence over them. We protest, then, against any influence which it may be thought woman exerts being taken as an equivalent for social equality. So very far are we for taking it as an equivalent, that we contend for social equality in the first place for its intrinsic justice; but in the second place because it would increase the influence of woman, and diminish that of man, by making her more independent and self-relying,—more energetic, less easily wrought upon, less passive in receiving influences, more active in making her own mind work upon and assimilate, for its own nourishment, those influences with which it does come into contact.

We shall be disposed to acknowledge that woman's influence has been sufficient to obtain her justice, when it has obtained for her, as we have no doubt it will, perfectly just and equal rights with the other sex. When this is the case, we shall expect to see each woman wakened up into a sense of her individual responsibilities and duties: finding herself no longer classed with children and idiots, we may reasonably expect to see her rousing herself up, and applying, with renewed energy, to all her duties; not only to her household affairs, but to the delightful task,— which her present flimsy and deficient education often hinders her from attempting at all, and still oftener when she does attempt it, interferes with the effective performance of—the training her children in the paths of wisdom and virtue. A more generally judicious performance of this duty will doubtless increase woman's influence; but the influence so exerted will be for the benefit of the whole human race, and can never, therefore, be given as a reason for depriving of civil rights those who exercise it; especially if we consider that the energy, independence, and self-reliance, which are necessary for its exertion, are themselves the fruits of social equality.

CHAPTER III.

ON THE USE OF THE TERM "WOMAN'S SPHERE."

> All constraint
> Except what wisdom lays on evil men,
> Is evil; hurts the faculties,—
> and begets
> In those that suffer it a sordid mind.
> *Cowper.*

Having thus, as briefly as possible, pointed out to our readers the most prevalent errors with regard to woman's influence, we proceed to call their attention to some other opinions, equally fallacious, with regard to the nature and extent of woman's sphere.

Woman's sphere is a phrase which has been generally used to denote the various household duties usually performed by her; but this is employing the phrase in a very limited sense, and one that requires explanation. Strictly speaking, a person's sphere comprises the whole range of his duties; but, taken in this limited sense, woman's sphere does not do this: for she has very many duties in common with man, besides those household requirements peculiar to her as a woman. The meaning usually attached to the phrase "duties of woman's sphere," would be much better expressed, were we to say, duties *peculiar* to woman's sphere. However, the phrase being an established one, we shall use it in its usual limited sense, having thus explained.

There is at present, we believe, almost every variety of sentiment on this subject, from the narrowest and most bigoted to the most extended and liberal; but we think that the three following classes of opinions will be found, without much straining, to comprehend them all.

1st. Those who think that woman's sphere really and truly comprises only her domestic duties, and that her mind ought never to stir beyond these.

2d. Those who think her mind ought to be enlarged, and her condition improved in some respects; but that she ought not to be equally privileged with man.

3d. Those who think she has a just claim to equal rights with man.

8

We do not speak to those who hold the first class of opinions, their prejudices being usually too obstinate and deep-seated for eradication; they in general maintain, that intellectual culture would take woman out of her proper sphere, that is, take her away from her domestic employments by raising her above them. Those who hold the second class maintain that woman may profitably cultivate her mind in literature, science, or even politics; they declare that a more substantial education, far from raising woman above her domestic duties, will both show her how important those duties are, and enable her to perform them much better. This class maintain of the possession of equal civil rights what the first do of a more enlightened education, that it would take woman out of her sphere. We ourselves hold, we hope with many more, that woman has a right to social equality; and we also maintain, that the possession of this just right would not interfere in the slightest with her domestic duties or "woman's sphere," as it is called. Nay, we go still farther, and assert, that the energy, self-reliance, and intelligence, which the possession of this right has such a tendency to foster and call into action, would be highly favourable to a more enlarged view of those duties and a more active discharge of them.

There is a class of writers, mostly feminine, who use this phrase very frequently; they are in general of the number of those who have escaped in a great measure from the thraldom of old prejudices with regard to woman. They have all of them outgrown in some degree, many of them altogether, the opinion, that with regard to woman it is best to "rear of ignorance the safe high wall;" but they seem to have almost a nervous apprehension of being thought to step out of woman's proper place themselves, or of trying to induce others to do so, when they advocate such comparatively new opinions as the following: that woman's nature is capable of, and would repay, as much cultivation as that of man; that it is quite allowable, and even highly proper that she should take an interest in politics, and try to influence all her friends towards her own side of the question. The consequence of this apprehension is, that these writers take every opportunity of deprecating the idea that their opinions have any tendency to take woman out of what they call her sphere.

I shall give a few passages to show how the phrase is generally used.

"We claim for them [women] no less an office than that of instruments (under God) for the regeneration of the world—restorers of God's image in the human soul. Can any of the warmest advocates of the political rights of women claim or assert for her a more exalted mission—a nobler destiny! That she will best accomplish this mission by moving in the sphere which God and nature have appointed, and not by quitting that sphere for another, it is the object of these pages to prove."*

"Women have a mission! ay, even a political mission of immense importance! which they will best fulfil by moving in the sphere assigned them by Providence; not comet-like, wandering in irregular orbits, dazzling indeed by their brilliancy, but terrifying by their eccentric movements and doubtful utility."†

"The blindness which sees not how these influences would be lessened by taking her out of the sphere assigned by Providence, if voluntary, is wicked,—if real, is pitiable."‡

"If anything urged in behalf of women tends to taking them out of their own sphere, I wish that it may be promptly and completely refuted; for nothing can be for the good of society, that is not built upon nature and reason."**

"Because it is perceived that women have a dignity and value greater than society or themselves have discovered; because their talents and virtues place them on a footing of equality with men, it is maintained that their present sphere of action is a contracted one, and that they ought to share in the public functions of the other sex. Equality, mental and *physical* is proclaimed! This is a matter too ludicrous to be treated anywhere but in a professed satire; in sober earnest, it may be asked upon what grounds so preposterous a doctrine is built up?"††

It appears to us that using the phrase "woman's sphere" in this manner, is simply a mere begging of the question. Of course, no one wishes to take her out of what he considers her true and proper sphere. We should think there could not be two opinions as to the propriety of her moving in the sphere which God and nature intended her to fill; the only difficulty is in deciding what that true and natural sphere is. As long as opinions are so various on that point, it is not very philosophical to

---

*   Woman's Mission.
†   Ibid.
‡   Woman's Mission.
** Woman's Rights and Duties.
†† Woman's Mission.

use the phrase as if its meaning were quite undisputed. Many people—
we are afraid the majority of the middle classes—think that woman's
duties are comprised in good humour and attention to her husband,
keeping her children neat and clean, and attending to domestic
arrangements. These would all most decidedly be of opinion, that the
authoresses, whom we have quoted, do wish to take woman out of what
they consider her proper sphere, when they encourage her to take an
interest in politics, and allow, that it is proper for them to influence their
friends in questions regarding public affairs. But whenever any one goes
a step further than these writers themselves, and expresses the opinion
that civil rights are quite consistent with—nay are almost necessary to—
the proper performance of all her other duties, nothing can surpass the
abhorrence with which they start back from so atrocious a doctrine! The
unhappy deluded creatures who entertain such opinions are, it seems,
unworthy of serious argument. It being decided, very conveniently, that
reason would be wasted upon them, they are treated to a mixture of a
little anger with a great deal of contemptuous pity. It is truly amusing to
see the superiority assumed over them by these writers, who can think
of no better means for reclaiming them from their low and lost estate
than bestowing upon them such appellatives as "fiery champions,"
"indiscreet advocates," &c.

But although the arguments on our side of the question are hardly
thought worthy of a serious refutation, yet our cause is thought
important enough to be worthy of misrepresentation. Because we think
that equality of rights is necessary to protect the weakness of woman
from the overbearing strength of man, we are said to proclaim mental
and *physical* equality! We were aware that many men, eminent for their
attainments in mental science, entertained the opinion of the intellectual
equality of the sexes; but we are yet to learn who has maintained their
physical equality. If any such fiery champions really do exist, they are
certainly both very few in number, and very little known to the public;
nor, if this be a fair specimen of their views, do they at all deserve to be
dragged from their well-merited obscurity.

In this little work*—the errors in which we are the more anxious to
point out, as it has had a wide circulation, and as we agree with the writer
in most of her details, keeping at the same time our opinion, that she has
rested them upon a most insufficient theory—the authoress, while
advocating more enlarged and comprehensive views of woman's duties,

* Woman's Mission.

is yet of opinion that the old prejudices with regard to the limited nature of those duties were in the main correct. She says:—

"As one atom of falsehood in first principle nullifies a whole theory, so one principle fundamentally true, suffices to obviate many minor errors. This fundamentally-true principle, I am prepared to show, exists in the established opinions concerning the true sphere of woman; and that, whether originally dictated by reason or derived from a sort of intuition, they are right, and for this cause: the one quality on which woman's influence and value depend, is the renunciation of self, and the old prejudices respecting her inculcated self-renunciation."

Now we would like to examine this a little; and in the first place would ask, What is self-renunciation? This question we shall answer by a quotation from Dr Channing.

"The truth is, that the human will never is so strenuous as in this act which is called the renunciation of itself, and by nothing does it more build up its own energy. The phrase means, that we would sacrifice inclination at the least suggestion of duty. But who does not know, that the mind never puts forth such strength of purpose, or will, as in overcoming desire? And what is the highest end and benefit of this warfare with desire? It is, that the mind may accumulate force of moral purpose, and that the will may more sternly, unconquerably, resolve on the hardest duties and sublimest virtues to which God may call us."

Such we take to be the true meaning of the term, often misapplied, of self-renunciation; a duty which all Christians, of whatever sex, are alike called upon to exercise; but whether this is the sort of self-renunciation which old usage exacts from woman we think very doubtful indeed. However, letting that pass for a moment, and allowing, for the sake of argument, that it is the proper sort of self-renunciation which old prejudice demands from woman, and that woman's value and influence depend upon that spirit; allowing this, still we insist that the writer of "Woman's Mission" has not proved all that is necessary to gain her point; she must also show, which she has not even attempted, that the proposed enlargement of woman's sphere is incompatible with the spirit of self-renunciation; and this is what we utterly deny. The wider the field of action, the wider also is the field for self-renunciation.

But to revert a little: we think that the old prejudices regarding woman convert the noble duty of self-renunciation into a most criminal self-extinction. These old prejudices extinguish her individuality, oblige her to renounce the good even more than the evil of her nature, and convert the inflexible rule of duty into a very flexible principle of submission to, and connivance at, all the weaknesses and wickednesses of man. No one will doubt this who has studied the *beau-ideal* of a wife in Chaucer's tale of Griselda, and which is, with some modification, too much the original character from which the good wife—having a bad husband—of modern story is taken. A woman is thought perfect if she is represented as continuing to love, with the most ardent and constant affection, a monster who first gained her love by guile, and then treated her in so brutal a manner as to merit the contempt of the whole world. The love which is felt for such a being, if real, is a blind passion which ought to be reprobated rather than admired; but if a conviction of duty induces it, it is a pity to see so noble a principle so ill directed.

True self-renunciation strengthens and invigorates the mind; but such self-extinction as old custom prescribes to woman enfeebles and debases it. No pure and noble-minded woman can long love affectionately, and submit passively to, a vicious and dissipated,—or even to a good and virtuous tyrant,—without having her own mind greatly deteriorated.

We believe that a great many of the loose and erroneous notions which people pick up, rather than acquire, regarding the nature of woman's duties, have their origin in the partial nature of the institutions of society with regard to her. Those institutions had their foundation, and were very valuable, in times of strife and danger, when might almost constituted right; but when a more peaceful state of society has succeeded—when we hope right will be found to constitute might—is it not proper to examine the legacy which these stormy days have left us, and see whether, in our present condition, it is worth retaining or not?

Our own opinion of the true and extensive nature of woman's sphere will be seen more clearly in the course of the following pages; we only wish in this place to show some of the most obviously groundless conclusions which have been arrived at on the subject, and that the phrase has as yet no definite, precise, and unmistakable meaning. Those who wish woman to stand still, accuse those who wish her to advance of the high misdemeanour of taking her out of her sphere: these deny the charge, but throw the same imputation on those again who wish to see woman more free and independent. These last also deny the obnoxious charge, being unable to see an incompatibility, which the others do not attempt to prove but take for granted, between the possession of civil rights, and the performance of household duties, any more than between the possession of civil rights and the performance of business duties.

For our own part we should be as sorry as any one to see the domestic virtues of woman impaired; but we see no shadow of fear that such a consequence must necessarily follow the success of the opinions which we advocate. The fireside virtues are not properly cultivated by a mere housewife.

"Well ordered home man's chief delight to make."

is a task which the accomplished woman can alone efficiently perform; she alone can make her fireside a scene of happiness and improvement to all who approach it; she alone can clearly show her children that the paths of wisdom and virtue are also those of pleasantness and peace; she alone will be as able and as solicitous to aid their mental development as to care for their physical comfort. All that unshackled self-dependence, all that freedom and elasticity of mind which social independence and equality, as we hope to convince the readers of the following pages, alone can thoroughly bestow, are not only favourable, but almost necessary to the right performance of those duties. Taking the phrase in its proper sense, we believe that the best and noblest of women will always find their greatest delight in the cultivation of the domestic virtues.

But although we are convinced that no elevation of the position of woman can ever withdraw domestic occupations and pleasures from forming a part, and perhaps even the chief part of her sphere, yet we are quite unable to see either the right or the reason which confines her to those occupations and pleasures. Nay! can any right be produced save that which is conferred by the strong right hand? Or any better reason than that it has been done from time immemorial?

There is yet another consideration connected with this subject worthy of our attention. If all woman's duties are to be considered as so strictly domestic, and if God and nature have really so circumscribed her sphere of action—What are we to think of the dreadful depravity of thousands upon thousands of unprotected females, who actually prefer leaving their only proper sphere, and working for their own subsistence—to starvation? Is it not shocking to see their consciences so seared that they are quite unaware of the dreadful nature of the course they are following? Ought not such wicked creatures to be exterminated? Or if we charitably allow them to cover their sins under the strong plea of necessity, what are we to think of that state of society which absolutely forces thousands of unfortunates to contradict their own nature—not by enlightening or enlarging their sphere—but by thrusting them entirely out of it? We say thrusting them entirely out, because we consider that domestic duties, though not occupying the whole of woman's sphere, ought always to form an integral part of it; and because few women are induced to work for themselves, except under the influence of such a pressure from without as obliges them to devote their whole time to any occupation they may choose, for obtaining subsistence, to the exclusion of course of all the peculiar duties of their sphere.

It may be said that this is merely an incidental evil—that it is a pity, but cannot be entirely avoided. Well! allowing that it is merely an incidental evil, still it is one which affects immense numbers of women; and if it is allowed to be in a great measure unavoidable, we would ask, is it fair to continue institutions which in their turn perpetuate those absurd prejudices which make it next to a certain loss of caste for any woman to attempt earning an honest and independent livelihood for herself? These prejudices have also had the very bad effect of limiting woman's choice of occupations to a few, and those the most tiresome and unhealthy of all the avocations which exist in the world.

We do not say, take away all occasion for woman being obliged to enter into an honourable and useful occupation; (for we think independence as necessary to the moral dignity of woman, as it confessedly is to that of man;) but we do say, either this must be done, or there is no excuse for not giving them as complete equality as law can give them. Even with perfectly fair play, they will still have plenty of difficulties to struggle with.

Putting, however, those cases out of the question, as exceptions to the general rule, where woman is forced to make what may be called unnatural exertions, and taking her in what is most certainly her natural, and we hope, also, her most frequent condition, that of a happy wife and mother, who requires to exert herself only to use judiciously the means supplied by her husband for their domestic comfort; still we say that this person's usefulness, even in the peculiar duties of her sphere, would not be at all impaired by her taking a more or less active interest, as her time might permit, in the welfare of her country.

Again we would repeat, that though no scheme would be of a healthy complexion the object or the consequence of which was to take woman away from domestic occupations, (or in other words, make woman change places with man, for one of them must attend to these matters,) so neither is there justice, to either sex, in the social system which tries to confine them to those occupations. We say tries, for it only succeeds in throwing obstacles in the way of woman's sphere being enlarged judiciously, and in a right direction.

We hope, then, that we have made it sufficiently clear to our readers, that the use of the phrase "woman's sphere," in the manner in which it generally is employed, is a mere gratuitous assumption by the writer who employs it, that his idea of the extent of woman's duties is the correct one; which, we confess, we are unreasonable enough to desire that he should prove rather than assume.

CHAPTER IV.

BUSINESS AND DOMESTIC DUTIES COMPARED.

"Nothing is more common than mistakes as to the comparative importance of the different vocations of life."—*Channing.*

Having thus attempted to point out to the attention of our readers the most obvious of those fallacies, by the assumption of which, as truths, the forcible cramping and confining of woman's sphere is attempted to be justified, we think it would very much assist us in this investigation, were we now to institute a comparison between domestic and business duties—these appearing to be the broad and distinct divisions into which the peculiar duties of the sexes separate—that we may see whether there is any truth in the very general impression, that woman's sphere is a mean one in comparison with man's; and that he requires both greater ability, and more cultivation of his natural capacity, to succeed in any of his usual avocations than woman does to succeed in her most usual avocation—the charge of a family.

This charge includes the superintendence of all the internal arrangements of the family, makes her the principal conductor of the fireside education of the children, and gives her a very great control over all the education they receive, moral, mental, or physical. In every case where the husband is engaged in business, the wife has at least the chief management of all these matters; and in very many cases has the sole charge of them.

The first division of the duties of the mistress of a family—the superintendence of the internal arrangements of it—requires a constant attention to order and economy. She must exert herself to set everything in such a train, as that all the work of the household shall go on in a smooth, orderly, and systematic manner, without either confusion or bustle; and she must be careful that no temptation induce her to allow her expenditure to exceed her income. She must use all her skill so to apportion the means at her command to the demands made upon them, that every want of her family conjointly, and of each individual of it separately, may be attended to in exact proportion to its real necessity.

17

Nice discrimination in weighing the relative importance of many different objects and assigning to each its proper value, and strict adherence to the judgment cautiously formed, require a very considerable exertion both of mental and moral power; and these are all called for in this—the lowest—department of the duties of the mistress of a family. But these duties, and the powers necessary for their discharge, sink into insignificance when we turn to the second division of the domestic duties of woman.

As chief conductor of the home education of her children, who can over-estimate the constant exercise of intelligence required by woman? And this intelligence is to be exerted not upon matter, but upon mind. It is to be employed not in the ordinary and coarse details of business, but in watching sedulously and assisting judiciously the unfolding of the youthful mind. It is to watch with the most unremitting care the development, in the mind of the child, of the good as well as the evil of human nature; and while it fosters every appearance of goodness with the warmest encouragement, it must repress every manifestation of evil with the tenderest yet firmest constancy. Nor is it alone over the morals of her children that a mother's care and tenderness ought to keep watch. She must assist and direct the development of the intellectual no less than the moral powers of those immortal beings whose earliest and most important years have been committed to her charge. Who can mark like her the first dawn of curiosity and intelligence in the infant mind, and feed and excite that curiosity in the manner best suited to that unfolding intelligence? And when the opening mind has made some progress towards maturity, who like a mother can excite so keen a thirst for knowledge, that the labour which is necessary to satisfy it—if it ever can be satisfied—seems a thousand times more attractive than all the trifling pleasures and gaieties of youth?

This is but a short account of woman's domestic duties; but we hope it will serve to show that the fulfilment of these duties is no such simple and easy matter as many thoughtlessly imagine. Their great importance may be seen by the terrible consequences of their neglect. By neglect of the first department, disorder and confusion will be introduced into the family affairs; and all the discomforts of poverty will be felt, even where there is more than sufficient means for comfort and enjoyment. And by neglect of the second department, the very springs of life are poisoned; and when these are embittered, how shall we sweeten the death-dealing waters of the fountain?

If we have been at all successful in imparting to our readers our own ideas of the nature of domestic duties, and the responsibilities which attach to their proper discharge, they will have no difficulty in acknowledging, that there is no degree of natural intellectual capacity, or of acquired knowledge and cultivation, which may not be engaged in these duties with perfect propriety, and without the shadow of misapplication or degradation.

Having come to this conclusion with regard to the domestic duties of woman, we would now turn our attention for a little to the inquiry,— whether an enlarged and enlightened understanding is more necessary for the discharge of the business duties of man? On the contrary, if we overlook the learned professions,—which of course occupy only a very small portion of the mass of men,—we shall find that no great exertion of the mental powers is required to perform the common run of business duties as well as they possibly can be performed. We have merely to mention a baker, a tailor, a shoemaker, in short, all sorts of tradesmen and shopkeepers, to make good our assertion. This is more especially the case, now that the division of labour is so rigidly practised that men often pass long periods of their business lives in the manufacture of little trifling things, in the construction of which they neither exert, nor are required to exert, any mental faculty whatever. Even when the result of a number of men's labour is a complicated piece of machinery, many of the men employed in constructing the different parts may find the complete machine as great an enigma as if they had had no share in the making of it. We have been credibly informed, that even in the professions which are based upon science, it is only the leading men who are required to exert much intellectual vigour; that the mediocre members of those professions serve an apprenticeship, get into a jog-trot routine of duty, do their work by the rules and tables of wiser heads, and are required to exert their mental faculties much less than is generally supposed.

To be very successful in any of the professions may require more firmness of nerve and more steady concentration of intellect than to manage a family with propriety; but certainly the proper management of a family infers the presence and constant exercise of those mental faculties, a greater concentration of which than usual is occasionally required in the learned professions. Neither are there any rules or tables which can materially assist woman in the performance of duties the features of which are so various and shifting: each woman must use her own judgment in her own case, and continually adapt her conduct to its changing phases.

Let it then be borne in mind, that that great power of mental endurance, that capability of long-continued intellectual labour, which is required for the attainment of great eminence in any of the professions, is not required for the successful pursuit of those occupations which must ever form the great staple of man's employments. If these things are acknowledged and borne in mind, we hope to carry our readers along with us in the opinion, that the domestic duties of the mass of women are more onerous, and require even greater mental exertion, than the duties connected with business of the mass of men.

It is very true, and we acknowledge it with sorrow, that levity and dissipation in the higher ranks; and in the lower the pressure of external circumstances, which often obliges the wife to leave her own particular province to assist her husband in his; and in all ranks the want of an invigorating and enlightened education interfere sadly with domestic occupations and duties. But considering simply the nature of those duties, and the powers required for performing them aright—without reference to whether they really are generally performed or not—we think it must be allowed, that tolerable ability and cultivation are necessary; and that the highest ability, and most extensive cultivation, would not be wasted in being applied to their discharge.

In connexion with this subject we shall quote a few passages from an essay of Dr Channing on education, which puts a part of woman's duties in the honourable light in which we wish them to appear.

"We maintain that higher ability is required for an educator of the young, than for being a statesman. The statesman must study and manage the passions and prejudices of the community; the educator must study the essential, the deepest, the loftiest principles of human nature. The statesman works with coarse instruments for coarse ends; the educator is to work by the most refined influences on that delicate ethereal essence—the immortal soul. Nothing is more common than mistakes as to the comparative importance of the different avocations of life. Noisy, showy agency, which is spread over a great surface, and therefore seldom penetrates beneath the surface, is called glory. How few reflect, that the greater man is he who, without noise or show, is wisely fixing in a few minds, broad, pregnant, generous principles of judgment and action, and giving an impulse which will carry them on for ever. According to these views, we think it a greater work to educate a child, in the true and large sense of the word, than to rule a state."

It is true that these remarks are more particularly applied to the professional teachers of youth; but a little consideration will show, that they may be applied, with even superior force, to parents, and especially to mothers. The training given at school is not the only, nor by any means the most important element in the education of youth. The mother's influence comes before the teacher's; and the impressions she makes are more permanent than his.

From whence, then, springs the great mistake, of supposing woman's sphere a mean and ignoble one? Why! from the very obvious cause, that its duties are not generally understood, and are therefore rarely performed,—the very same cause which, in past times, occasioned the low estimate of the duties of a teacher. When duties are not perceived with some degree of clearness and precision, it is almost the same as if they did not exist. If they are not seen at all, of course they cannot be performed; and if they are only indistinctly seen, they cannot be well performed. Now, in general, woman does not see, or sees only indistinctly—we are well aware that there are many noble exceptions—the wide field for exertion contained within her own peculiar sphere; and her practice, even when she does aim at performance of duty, is of course limited by the contracted nature of her vision. Thus the value of her duties comes to be measured by her performance of them, rather than by their natural and intrinsic worth. And it is thus that household duties, and the charge of a family, come to be considered as contemptible occupations, which any ignorant or foolish woman is quite competent to undertake. Nor is woman alone to blame in this matter. The proud contempt of man for these unobtrusive but important duties, and the moral blindness of woman, have mutually reacted upon, and reproduced each other; so that man must at least share in the blame attached to woman's errors in this respect.

We trust that our readers will now be prepared to conclude with us, that it is impossible that the being in whom is placed so great, so noble a trust, should be possessed of so mean and shallow an intellect that enlightenment and elevation would only render her giddy! No! this cannot be believed, when the nature of her trust is understood, and its value justly appreciated. We may certainly rest assured that the duties imposed, and the powers granted for their discharge, bear some better proportion to each other, than these contemptuous opinions of woman would lead us to suppose.

B

CHAPTER V.

WOMAN'S CLAIM TO EQUAL RIGHTS.

"To see one half of the human race excluded by the other from all participation of government, is a political phenomenon which, according to abstract principles, it is impossible to explain." — *Talleyrand.*

We shall now proceed to enumerate more precisely the disadvantages which, in this country, we conceive woman in general labours under. The principal of these seem to be:—

I.   Want of equal civil rights.

II.   Enforcement of unjust laws.

III.   Want of means for obtaining a good substantial education.

The second and third of these grievances are, in themselves, and essentially, evil and unjust. The first is, perhaps, principally of importance, because without it there are no sure means of obtaining and securing the others; but although the results of legislative powers are what render those powers chiefly desirable, still they are also desirable on their own account; free institutions being one of the most important and elevating influences which can be brought to bear on the human mind. We, therefore, place the deprivation of civil rights first; being the fertile source of many other evils, as well as most injurious in itself.

The ground on which equality is claimed for all men is of equal force for all women; for women share the common nature of humanity, and are possessed of all those noble faculties which constitute man a responsible being, and give him a claim to be his own ruler, so far as is consistent with order, and the possession of the like degree of sovereignty over himself by every other human being. It is the possession of the noble faculties of reason and conscience which elevates man above the brutes, and invests him with this right of exercising supreme authority over himself. It is more especially the possession of an inward rule of rectitude, a law written on the heart in indelible characters, which raises him to this high dignity, and renders him an accountable being, by impressing him with the conviction that there are certain duties which he owes to his fellow-creatures. Whoever possesses this consciousness, has also the belief that the same convictions of duty are implanted in the breast of each member of the human family. He feels that he has a *right* to have all those duties exercised by others towards him, which his conscience tells him he ought to exercise towards others; hence the natural and equal rights of men.

We do not mean to enter into the question of the claim of all men to equal rights, but simply to state the foundation on which that claim rests, and to show that the first principles on which it does rest apply to all mankind, without distinction of sex. The question of the equal right of all men to be represented in the Legislature, would be the more out of place here, as it has already been ably discussed, and answered in the affirmative, by many of the greatest men of modern times: of these, Jeremy Bentham may be mentioned as the chief. Now, as all the arguments of those who may be called Benthamites apply equally to men and women,* (with the exception of some counter objections in the case of woman, which we shall examine and show to be but trifling,) being built upon the grand characteristics of human nature, which are the same in both sexes, it is certainly inconsistent to allow those arguments weight in the case of the one sex, and refuse it in that of the other. Perhaps those who refuse their assent to these doctrines—who cling to expediency, and put *right* altogether out of the question, are, to a certain length, excusable for denying equal civil rights to woman; but even these would find it difficult to assign any reason in favour of the expediency which they assert exists for the exclusion of *all* women from this right.

Our readers will, doubtless, soon observe, that throughout all the arguments we have used in these pages runs the idea of the equal right of all men to be represented—actually and really represented—in Parliament. Now, this has been merely because we were not exactly aware of the grounds on which this privilege has been confined to persons having a house of ten-pounds' rent and upwards. Of course, we do not mean that all women should possess a privilege which has, as yet, only been conferred on particular classes of men; we only mean to insist

---

* The passage in which Bentham has recorded his conviction, that all his tests of aptitude for political privileges apply equally to both sexes, is rather long for extraction; but it has been well condensed by the editor of the original edition of his works.

"On the admission of females, Mr Bentham's plan forbore to lay much stress; because it found no grounds for any very determinate assurance that, in that case, the result would be materially different; and because no minds could be expected to be at present prepared for it. *But it declared that it could find no reasons for exclusion,* and that those who, in support of it, gave a sneer or a laugh for a reason, because they could not find a better, had no objection to the vesting of absolute power in that sex, and in a single hand: so that it was not without palpable inconsistency and self-condemnation, that the exclusion they put upon this class could be brought forward."—*Ed. of original Edition of Bentham.*

that the right is the same in both sexes. If there be any particular reason for the exclusion from this privilege of a certain class among men, we would allow it to have weight for excluding the corresponding class of women, but for these alone. We would insist that, with whatever speciousness certain classes among men have been excluded from this right, it does not follow as a matter of course—as often assumed—that *all* women ought to be excluded. The class of women corresponding to the privileged class among men have still a claim; and the *onus probandi* against them lies with those who advocate the continuance of the system of exclusion.

The exercise of those rights would be useful in two ways: it would tend to ennoble and elevate the mind; and it would secure the temporal interest of those who exercise it.

No doubt can be entertained of the debasing nature of slavery. Its tendency to crush and extinguish the moral and spiritual, and to elevate the animal in human nature, is now generally acknowledged; but it does not seem to be so clearly perceived, that every degree of constraint partakes of the same tendency. Perfect liberty, we should say, is that which allows as much freedom to each individual human being, as is consistent with the same degree of freedom in every other human being. Everything short of this liberty, however far it may be from absolute slavery, yet partakes of its nature, and of its power of crushing, cramping and debasing the human mind; of implanting a slavish spirit, and of substituting cunning for true wisdom. It prevents the human being from developing its powers; forbids independence of thought and action, without which there can be no virtue; and exercises, in a thousand baneful ways, the most pernicious influence on the formation of individual character. What a cramping and keeping-down effect on the mind of women must this remark have, "What have women to do with that?"—the matter in question being one of interest to the whole human family,—"let them mind their knitting, or their house affairs!" Now, this remark is, perhaps, only occasionally expressed in words, yet the spirit of it runs through all society: if not often *spoken* in conversation, it is constantly acted on by our institutions.

Not only does civil liberty remove those evil influences, but it also substitutes ennobling influences in their place. The consciousness of responsibility which the possession of a vote would bestow, the dignity of being trusted, the resolution to justify the faith placed in her truth and judgment, would all call forth, in woman, noble powers which, hitherto, have been too much suffered to lie dormant: powers which, when they have occasionally peeped forth in an individual, have but too often been greeted with laughter and ridicule, sometimes even with more serious obloquy. Thus, some of the gifted among women have been induced to hide their light beneath an exterior of levity and frivolity, while others have gained the pardon of the lord of the creation for encroaching on what he claims as his peculiar domain—the intellectual—by falling down and worshipping him, and then devoting their talents to instructing their sex in all the duties of this idolatry. The possession of the franchise would tend to raise woman above the bonds of this intolerable restraint; would give free play to her faculties, energy and individuality to all her powers. It would remove that inert and subdued state of mind which must be the result of a belief, that one is not fit for this or that thing of common sense and every-day life.

But, besides all this, equal privileges are necessary for the mere temporal interests of all; for no one can be supposed to know so well as the individual himself, what is for his own peculiar advantage. Accordingly, it is found, that when one class legislates for any other class, it attends first to the bearing of that legislation on its own class interests; not, perhaps, so much from selfishness, (although that also will help to blind the legislator,) as because it *knows* what is for its own interest better than it possibly can know the interest of another class with whose mode of life, and consequent wants and wishes, it never can be so familiar as with its own. Each class, then, knowing what is best for its own peculiar benefit, will have its interests best attended to by its own representative; and when all are represented, those measures will be resolved on which favour the happiness of the greatest number.

We are aware that it is said, that woman is virtually represented in Parliament, her interests being the same as those of man; but the many laws which have been obliged to be passed to protect them from their nearest male relatives, are a sufficient answer. The simple fact of such laws being necessary, would be a strong presumption that woman requires to have her interests really represented in the Legislature; but the manifestly unjust nature of the laws which this necessity has produced, convert presumption into proof, by showing most distinctly, that no sentiment, either of justice or gallantry, has been sufficient to ensure anything like impartiality in the laws between the sexes. Those laws, then, are in themselves a convincing proof, first, that woman requires representation, and, second, that she is not represented. So utterly unjust are they,—as we shall show when treating more particularly of the subject,—that no real representative of woman could have any share in the making of them. They are evidently the production of men legislating for their own most obvious interests, (I say obvious, because their own true and deep interest was to do justice,) without the slightest reference to the injustice they were committing against women.

Members of Parliament are so deeply engaged with the party-spirit of politics, that the more special interests of woman, even although most intimately bound up with the general prosperity and wellbeing of the race, are in great danger of being entirely lost sight of. Unless she be actually represented, there is very little chance of woman's obtaining justice, even in those matters where the laws are acknowledged to be partial,—the evident results of class legislation. The justice of her complaints may be allowed; but if she has no one whose business it is to advocate her cause, its justice will hardly prevent it from being laid on the shelf. It is a proverbial saying, that "everybody's business is nobody's business;" and this is very well exemplified in the manner in which woman is pretended to be represented now.

Denying that women are represented, infers another great wrong done them. No taxation without representation, is the great motto of the British constitution. Does the tax-gatherer pass the door of the self-dependent and solitary female? Do the various commodities she consumes, come to her charged only with the price of their production and carriage to her? Or is a fourth, or even a third, added to that price, which goes into the public treasury? If she must pay, why cannot she also vote?

We have never seen any attempt to justify this deprivation of the civil rights of woman, on the footing of right or principle. And when we come to examine them, we hope we shall be able to impress our readers with our own opinion, that there is very little force in those arguments by which it has been thought to lodge itself so securely in the stronghold of expediency.

The indefinite, shadowy, unsubstantial grounds on which the privileges woman at present enjoys, rest, show that principle has little to do with them. It is in consideration of their common, moral, and accountable nature, that men have a natural claim to equality of rights; now, man and woman, however they may differ in some minor points of character, resemble each other in the grand features of both being moral and responsible beings. If, then, woman's rights are not the same as those of man, what are they? Do those who deny her title to equal rights, mean to assert that she has no rights whatever? If she has some, yet not the same rights, what are they? and on what grounds do they

26

rest? Let us try and have them clearly defined, and the reasons given, why they are not the same with those of man. An inquiry of this kind will, we think, show that all the privileges she at present enjoys are yielded merely in courtesy. They have no solid foundation whatever in any fixed principle. Many of them are accorded her simply of the good-will of the individuals who compose society, and would be refused her according to the strict letter of the law; for the laws represent an older stage of prejudice against her than is general now, although, from the want of any one to advocate her cause, the old laws are still allowed to continue in force.

A little inquiry will show, that there must be some very curious and inconsistent ideas prevalent about the civil duties for which women are fit or not fit,—for they are by no means even at present excluded from all civil privileges. The necessary property qualification admits her to vote for an East India Director; nor have we heard the faintest hint of any inconvenience resulting from the practice. What great and obvious difference there is between voting for the governors of India and those of England—so great and so obvious as to make the one a matter of course for women, the other an absurdity which cannot be so much as named without exciting the most contemptuous laughter—we confess we do not very clearly see. Nor is it alone in the government of that foreign country that women, equally with the other sex, are allowed a voice. In the local governments of our own country we often see women invested with a vote for some one or other of the public servants. Now, since no practical inconvenience has been found to result from allowing her to vote, for instance, for a commissioner of police—and since, in theory, it seems no more than justice—why not allow her right of voting for other local authorities, or any authorities whatever? why, in short, hinder her from voting on any public affair, when she can produce the only qualification that would be required from any one of the other sex? The very circumstance of woman holding and exercising such powers as these, without exciting any remark, shows that she is capable of exercising some civil rights without the least disturbance or confusion. And if this is the case now with even one of the rights of citizenship, who can say that in time it may not be the case with all?

It is said, in *Woman's Rights and Duties*, that "woman has a right to all the self-government she can exercise without interfering with man's convenience." But this right amounts to absolutely nothing, or worse than nothing; for it has an appearance of being something, while, in reality, it is but a phantasm, which one attempts in vain to grasp. Man must always, of course, be the judge of what is his own convenience: and what shadow of liberty does this bondage to man's convenience allow to woman? To leave the liberty of one-half of the human race at the mercy of the convenience of the other, amounts to an annihilation of the rights of that half. The proposition requires only to be mentioned in unadorned language that its injustice may be seen.

On the other hand, it must be borne in mind that equality of rights by no means implies perfect equality of authority. No difference of natural ability or of acquired knowledge between two men of the same rank makes any difference between the civil rights of those two men; yet it is easy to see that the character of both will be thrown into the scale, and that the man of ability will exercise his rights with an authority and weight in which the other will be totally deficient. The man of talent is not then sacrificed; because all of the same rank in society—however various in intellect and knowledge—have the same civil rights. No! he retains all the advantages of his mental superiority, and, in spite of the perfect equality of their rights, enjoys all that preëminence above his fellows, which that superiority naturally gives him. This seems to be the best illustration of the rights of woman. It is unjust to deprive her of equal, civil, and legal rights with man; but it is absurd to think, if she be really inferior in strength of body and mind, that the granting her those rights can ever do away with her subordination to man, or make her in every respect equal to him. It may as well be said, that the wise and foolish, learned and ignorant, industrious and idle, are all perfectly equal, because their civil rights are so.

We hope, then, it will be plain, that by asserting the natural equality of all reasonable human beings, we do not at all mean to advocate any irrational system of levelling, such as that the poor have a right to share equally the property of the rich. We should as soon think of insisting that the plain-looking, or the sickly, had an equal right to beauty and health with the handsome and the strong; yet such is the absurd meaning usually attached to equality. Neither do we mean to assert, that man and woman are strictly the same in their nature, or the character of their minds; but simply, that in the grand characteristics of their nature they are the same, and that where they differ, it is in the minor features; that they resemble far more than they differ from each other. And by equality, we mean equal, civil, and legal rights; such an equality as will prevent the rich or wise man from having more power over his fellow-creatures, than his riches or his wisdom naturally give him. And from

28

this rule we can see no reason whatever for excluding the female half of the human race. The weaker they are, the greater is their need of equal rights, that they may not fall under the tyranny of the stronger portion of their race. Besides all their natural disadvantages, they have at present a heavy artificial weight to keep them down in the scale of society. If that weight were taken off, they would only rise to their natural level in society, not one inch above it.

It is said, that this change would introduce disorder, and subvert all subordination,—that it would be sacrificing the strong to the weak; but this is a very groundless fear. If really more vigorous and powerful, both of body and mind, than woman, man must ever retain the ascendency. From what, then, springs the apprehension, that justice to woman would be followed by insubordination on her part, is hard to say. For our part, we cannot even understand why these things are feared. Female domination seems to our mind a chimera of the most fanciful kind. We are afraid that this argument is used more with the view of throwing ridicule upon the just claims of woman, than from any serious idea of its force.

But if we reject, on the one hand, the idea of female domination as ridiculous and absurd, so we must equally reject, on the other hand, the idea, that the boundary of woman's rights is to be found in the arbitrary convenience of man. Is it said, that woman was made for man and was born to obey him? We answer, Yes! it is true that woman was made for man, but not without reference to herself. Indeed, we insist, that the more she looks to her own nature, and serves that faithfully, the better will she answer the other end of her being, and show the more clearly, that she was indeed made for man. According to the present system, she is often anything rather than a helpmate for him, or he for her. Again, it is evident, that if woman is a responsible being, there must be a limit to her submission and obedience to man. If she is bound implicitly to obey, without reference to her own convictions of right and wrong, she cannot, as a matter of course, be held responsible for her actions; these proceeding not from her own free will, but the imperative commands of another. Accordingly, we find that obedience is not the first and highest duty of woman. She is bound, in common with man, to inquire diligently into all the duties of her position, and to pursue those duties sedulously; and were she commanded by father, brother, or husband, to do anything inconsistent with her ideas of rectitude, she would most obviously be wronging her own conscience were she to neglect its whispers for the more clamorous orders of her relatives. We agree at once that woman is bound to obey; but only when obedience does not contradict her own convictions of duty. So that evidently her obligation as a rational and responsible creature—to judge for herself—goes before her duty as a woman to obey her husband in all things not contrary to her own conscience.

Much of the unhappiness of domestic life is the consequence of the very mistaken idea, that implicit obedience is the duty of woman. This idea gives man such a high idea of his own prerogatives, that a woman, unless she be very fortunate in her connexions, is forced either openly to rebel, or else cringe and fawn for the sake of peace. It is the duty of servants to obey their employers, as well as wives to obey their husbands; but the obedience of both these classes is quite subordinate to their other moral duties, and is in fact the lowest of them all; and why? Simply for the very good reason, that all their other moral duties are sanctioned by that inward monitor which cannot direct them wrong; whereas this is embodied in the commands of a mortal always weak and often erring: of course, then, whenever they unfortunately come into contact, the latter must and ought to give way.

More definite ideas as to how far woman's obedience ought to extend—it being evident that it cannot be unlimited—would remove at least one of the many prevailing influences which are so hostile to domestic happiness. At present, woman being told she is to obey, and feeling that she cannot obey in all things, is but too apt, having once overstepped the line, to resist in all things, or at least not so much where she *ought* to resist, as where she *can* do so with a prospect of success. Hence either continual dissension, or a hen-pecked husband. But were it clearly understood that woman's obedience is a secondary duty, that she is bound in the first place to consult her moral nature, and only to obey when obedience is in accordance with her convictions of rectitude; then willing obedience, whenever conscience did not interfere, might be expected with more reason than it is now. And we may add, that in that case man would much more rarely seek obedience where woman could not grant it.

Hitherto, however, male writers have been too well satisfied with the mysterious nature of man's prerogatives to express this clearly; and female writers have been but too apt to truckle to the most powerful,—or else, which is perhaps the true reason, the universal subjection of women has extended to the minds even of the highly-gifted of that sex. We hope, however, that these indefinite and unsatisfactory ideas of the duties of the softer sex may soon give place to clearer views; that the proper limits of submission and obedience may be drawn, and woman's full rights accorded her. In that case, the subordination being consistent with reason, would have more chance of being cheerfully submitted to; while the authority of man would run less risk of degenerating into oppression.

Having thus attempted to show, that although in one sense woman was made for man, yet in another and higher she was also made for herself; and that the more faithful she is to the higher end of her being, the development of her whole nature moral and rational, the better will she fulfil the lower one, of ministering to the happiness of man. I shall now try to find out whether there is any need of so many artificial distinctions between the sexes, or whether we might not safely rely on their natural distinctions for retaining each in its proper place.

The most striking difference between the sexes is in their relative proportion of bodily strength, the frame of man being always much stronger than that of woman. And since the physical structure of man is stronger than that of woman, and the mental powers are manifested through physical organs, there is a strong presumption that man must always exceed woman in force of mind as well as in strength of limb. Accordingly the contrast between the minds of the different sexes is of the same nature as that between their physical constitutions. The one sex is soft, gentle, yielding; the other hard, stern, severe. The mental, like the physical organization of woman, seems more delicate than that of man; her mind, like her body, is less capable of long-continued or severe labour. But in estimating the difference between the sexes in point of intellectual vigour, there is great danger of rating woman too low. To prevent this, it is necessary to bear in remembrance, that the mind of woman never has been cultivated in the same degree as that of man; so that it is hardly possible to institute a fair comparison between them. The long course of neglect or scorn which has been the general fate of the female mind, must have repressed and deteriorated its powers. Although, therefore, we see that woman is at present inferior in vigour of mind, and may presume that she always must continue to be so in some respect, yet, on the other hand, it must also be admitted, that the partiality which has given so much greater an amount of mental cultivation to man than to woman, and the greater calls which he has had for exertion, have made this difference much greater than it would naturally be, were the same amount of culture and the same opportunities of exertion bestowed on both sexes.

Even when most cultivated, there is a degree of roughness and rudeness to be found in the mind of man when compared with that of woman, which is perhaps inseparable from its superior strength. This difference is well seen in the parental character. However fond a father may be of his child, he would be teazed and tormented by the constant watchfulness and attention which is necessary for its wellbeing, and which it is the delight of the mother to bestow. Her constant, patient, and cheerful attention to minutiæ, would certainly require from him a much greater effort than from her, and would fatigue him much more than a very considerable exertion either of body or mind. Woman must always of course continue to be the mother of the human race; and as no change in her condition can alter that law of nature, so neither can any change alter those peculiarities of her mental constitution which so nicely fit her for the duties of the maternal character. This character, the duties attendant upon it, and the peculiarities, mental and physical, which are required by it, is the great guarantee that the distinction between the sexes can never be lost by any equalization of their rights.

It will be readily allowed that, in the great essentials of their nature, man and woman are the same. They are alike moral, accountable, and immortal beings; and it is on this account that they are entitled to the same rights. But we hope it will also be seen, that there are so many minor differences in their characters as to render it almost absurd to imgaine that any elevation of woman's character or position could possibly derange the social economy. In short, all those differences from man in the character of woman, which are usually produced as reasons for depriving her of civil rights, weigh, with us, quite on the other side of the question, and force us irresistibly to the conclusion, that as there are so many natural differences between man and woman, there is no occasion for those artificial distinctions which had their foundation in the superior strength of man when war and spoil were the order of the day. Surely those differences, so strongly marked, may be allowed to do away with the fear of any violent convulsion, in the event of women receiving all the privileges of rational and responsible creatures. The peculiar characteristics of the sexes, show them so fitted to play into each other's hands, that I cannot conceive the idea of their interests ever interfering with each other. It is certainly the true interest of each to help the other forward as much as possible, and of both to assist in every way in advancing the cause of truth and liberty.

CHAPTER VI.

OBJECTIONS EXAMINED.

"As to persons of this sex, the sex in which the half, more or less, of the whole species is contained—usually, if not constantly, have they on this occasion been passed over without notice: an omission which, under a Mahometan government might have place with rather less prejudice to consistency than under a Christian one."—*Jeremy Bentham.*

In proceeding to consider some of the most common objections against this change, it must be borne in mind that there is no reform against which it is not very easy to produce objections. But in arguing against any reform, it is not enough to show that there are objections to it,—it must be shown that the objections against it are greater than the advantages which would arise from granting it.

The first objection I shall notice is, want of sufficient leisure: it may be said that woman has not time to spare from her domestic duties. In answering this objection, I shall, first, merely mention the case of those immense numbers of women who are forced to find time from their peculiarly domestic avocations to earn a subsistence for themselves and their families; and that other large class who have no domestic duties whatever, or, at least, none that can be pretended fully to occupy their time. These classes comprehend such great numbers of women, that they ought not to be put out of the question. But, large though they be, we must at present simply remind you of them,—then, leaving them as exceptions, consider the case of those who form the rule with regard to female avocations. Let us take then, as an example, a woman who has received a good substantial education, by which her mind has been both refined and strengthened. Let us suppose that she has no occasion to support herself; that she has a household and children to attend to; and, let me ask, are puddings and pies, roasting and boiling, dusting and washing, or even the rearing and educating her children, so entirely to engross her attention, that her heart and mind can never expand beyond her own little domestic circle? Nay, if her mind never does so expand, will she be able properly to regulate the concerns even of that little circle? Is she never to have a moment to spare—never a thought or a wish to bestow on the state of society around her? No: this certainly

33

ought not to be the case. Every family bears some relation—be it nearer or more remote—to every other family. No household, therefore, can, without blame, shroud itself up entirely in its own peculiar little concerns. A woman's family and domestic affairs ought to occupy her in the same degree that a man's business does him; but not a bit more exclusively. An extensive business does not prevent a man from giving some of his attention to the state of affairs in his town, neighbourhood, and country: neither ought a large family to prevent a woman doing the same. Indeed, the woman who shows most discretion in the management of her own matters, and pays most assiduous attention to her own peculiar duties, be they ever so complicated, will generally have some time to spare for the benefit of others. And, certainly, such a woman *ought* always to have more time to spare than is required for the judicious and conscientious discharge of the duties of one of the constituents of a Town Councillor and M.P.

Allowing, however, for the sake of argument, that if a woman has the rearing and training of a large family to attend to, she may be permitted to urge that as an excuse for confining her attention to her family alone. Still the time often, we may say always, comes, when her children leave her to settle themselves in the world; and then this excuse vanishes away. She now returns—and we revert with her—to that large class whose domestic affairs cannot be pretended fully to occupy their time; and, when this period arrives, is the formerly active and busily engaged mind to sink into inactivity and sloth? or is it to be forced to waste its energies in going about from house to house, engaged in tittle-tattle, gossiping, and scandal? Why is she to be debarred *now* from exercising her mind in any manner which the turn of that mind may direct or incline her to pursue?

The next objection we shall notice, is the fear that mixing in any degree in those weighty affairs may quite take away the relish for more domestic matters. But these so-much-despised domestic matters, are really as important to the happiness of the human race as the duties attached to civil rights; and they lie too near the heart of woman ever to be neglected, in any great degree, even were they the most insignificant affairs conceivable. It sometimes happens that a merchant, manufacturer, or shopkeeper, runs mad with politics, and leaves his own business neglected, that he may have leisure to attend to that of the nation; yet, to prevent more mishaps of that kind, nobody proposes to take away the civil rights of merchants, manufacturers, or shopkeepers. Now, the domestic duties of woman being so much more closely, or at least more immediately, bound up in the affections than the business duties of man, there is much less risk of her ever falling into such an error. Is it to be so much as imagined, that any political excitement will be so apt to make a woman forget her children as to make a man forget his counting-house, counter, or spinning-jennies? Every heart, worthy of the name, answers distinctly, and at once, No.

It may be objected, that such an introduction into the bustle of public life would injure the most charming characteristics of woman,—her gentleness and modesty. What a tax is this upon the conduct of men in their intercourse with each other! Does it appear that their business habits are so rough that they are afraid to allow of women mingling with them, lest they should lose their natural gentleness, and become as uncouth and as uncultivated as themselves! Why! let them mend their manners, and the difficulty at once disappears. However, even although this mode of getting rid of the obstacle should not be approved of by those who alone can put it into practice, we have no doubt that gentleness and modesty are too deeply rooted in the very constitution of woman to be so easily lost. We incline rather to hope that both parties may soon be improved by some amalgamation of manners—that women shall soon cease to be so soft and helpless, and men so rough and bearish. Having no fear that they can ever lose their distinctive marks, we confess we would like to see them approach each other a little nearer in character.

An objection something similar to the last is, that delicacy and decorum would suffer materially by the success of the opinions we advocate. The writer in *The Edinburgh Review*,* upon whose performance we shall have occasion to make so many comments, uses this objection as an argument for justifying the exclusion of women from hearing the debates in parliament. As women can always read the debates and proceedings of parliament, this exclusion is in itself an exceedingly trifling grievance; so trifling, that we should not have thought it worth naming, did we not fear that the spirit which dictated this petty insult is essentially the same as that which dictates their exclusion from more important privileges. As we are of opinion that the common ideas about female delicacy and decorum are far from correct, and as this writer seems to us to favour these ideas, we propose examining the excuse he makes for the exclusion of women from hearing the debates in parliament.

"Subjects must sometimes come under discussion which could not

* April, 1984, "Rights and Condition of Women."

be mooted before a female audience, without shocking that nice sense of decorum which now prevails in refined society, and which no right-minded person can wish to render less sensitive. It is true that the probable nature of the debate may sometimes be sufficiently known beforehand, to allow the usual occupants of the Ladies' Gallery the opportunity of absenting themselves. But this cannot always be the case. Subjects, such as we have alluded to, will be introduced incidentally and unexpectedly. They may be of deep importance; and such as no fastidious delicacy ought to prevent a member of parliament who values as he ought the responsibility which attaches to his situation, and the obligation which rests on him to do his duty fearlessly and frankly, from stating as clearly and forcibly to the House, as if his words were to be heard by no ears but those of men. In such a case it is not right that any one should be subjected to a painful struggle between the refined and decorous feelings of a British gentleman and the solemn and imperative duties of a British legislator."

We suppose that the above alludes to those terrible disorders and desperate vices of society, a fearful and shuddering glimpse of which is all that her own ideas of propriety allow to a modest woman; and, if such be the case, we cannot help thinking that a better acquaintance with those dreadful evils, and even great efforts to amend them, are perfectly consistent with female delicacy: to the pure all things are pure. The possession of a truer and more complete knowledge on this painful subject, by women in general, would do more to lessen the numbers of the most unfortunate outcasts of society—many of them more sinned against than sinning—than all the secret discussions of the House of Commons. However pleasant it may be for women themselves to intrench themselves in decorum and refinement from so painful a knowledge, and however consonant such behaviour may be to the prejudices of society,—yet such is not the manner in which those terrible disorders can be remedied. It certainly seems to us that there are no vices so desperate that they ought not to be unfolded to female eyes, of which females are themselves the partakers and most miserable victims. However painful the discussion of such subjects may be—and painful they must ever be to every refined and delicate mind whether male or female—yet, since the discussion is necessary, it ought not to be shrunk from. Since females are also even more interested than males in the suppression of those evils, we can see no propriety whatever in endeavouring to keep them in ignorance of their existence.

Is a woman one instant so perfect that vice is not even to be mentioned in her hearing; and the next—fallen perhaps through her very ignorance of evil—such a monster that her condition cannot be mentioned to her more virtuous or more fortunate sisters? No! had she been taught—at the expense, doubtless, of some painful but salutary shocks to her delicacy—the usual consequences moral and physical of the step she was about to take, she would never have gone near, far less gone over the fatal precipice.

> Vice is a monster of such hideous mien,
> As, to be hated, needs but to be seen.

All women will doubtless have their feelings shocked by listening to, or learning in any manner such sorrowful truths as those alluded to; but the really modest and virtuous will remain as pure as before; and those who are only fortunate in not having been much exposed to temptation, will see the danger of yielding to it when it does present itself. We think, then, that more knowledge on this subject would be very favourable to female morals, and not at all unfavourable to genuine delicacy. Nor can we think the subject unbecoming the thoughts or the pen of a woman, when we consider that those disorders involve, in the utmost degradation and misery, thousands and thousands of her own sex.

Innocence and virtue, though totally different, are often mistaken for the same thing. Innocence is hardly to be found in this world; our specimens of it are to be seen in the lamb, the dove, and the infant: it consists in ignorance of evil. Virtue is alone attained through a knowledge both of good and evil, and a determined strife against the latter in all its forms. The innocence of this world may often go astray from very ignorance. Virtue knows both the good and evil path, but adheres firmly to the former. Virtue, then, is by far the nobler attainment of the two.

It will be seen, in the passage I have quoted, that it is not the wounding of female delicacy that is feared. No: it is the pain that would be inflicted on the "refined and decorous" feelings of our present "British Legislators." Now we cannot but think that there is considerable affectation in absorbing such feelings to such persons; confusion they would be likely to feel,—but it is more probable that it would proceed from a guilty conscience than from true modesty. That refinement and delicacy of feeling which is coexistant with vice, deserves no great sympathy; we care little how much it is wounded, and would rejoice to see it altogether destroyed. We are none of those who think that vice loses half its evil by losing all its grossness. We would much rather it would show itself in its native deformity, that it might be hated as it deserves.

In the present confused and uncertain state of opinion with regard to female propriety and delicacy, we expect that many will dissent from the sentiments we have here expressed, especially those who hold, that any degree of publicity—such as authorship—is incompatible with female delicacy. We think that if such persons were to turn their attention to the state of manners and literature in former times—even no further back than the last century—their opinions would undergo some alteration. Surely it must be allowed by every one that, with regard to propriety and decorum, we have greatly improved, and are steadily improving upon the example of former ages. Now we think it can hardly be doubted, that this is in a very great measure owing to the increased freedom with which women come out into society, their more easy and familiar intercourse with men, their mixing more readily in literary circles, and even themselves becoming authors. These circumstances mutually act and react upon each other; an increase of propriety in public feeling enables woman to throw off some of the chains which bind her. Glad to do so, she mingles more freely in social intercourse; and this increased familiarity of association produces still further improvement, which she again, wisely and naturally, avails herself of. Thus, a modest and delicate woman of the present day can do a thousand things with perfect propriety which would have been quite inadmissible in her great-grandmother; and there may be a great many things quite inadmissible for her at present, which yet shall be perfectly proper for her granddaughter.

Surely, then, none but the deeply-prejudiced will refuse to acknowledge that women, by being instrumental in bringing about so happy a change, have both benefited their country and done honour to themselves. Had any false delicacy prevented them coming forward as they have done, our improvement in this matter would doubtless have been greatly retarded. How much more truly delicate was it, then, for women to mix in that society and engage themselves with that literature which they have assisted so much to purify, than it would have been for them to have shrunk from publicity, and so doing injury both to themselves and the community! Their own delicacy of mind was not impaired, while the decorum of society was greatly improved.

> ——"Good, the more
> Communicated more abundant grows,
> The author not impaired, but honoured more."

We hope, then, that our readers will be disposed to regard this objection as a frivolous one, and to come to our conclusion, that virtue would be improved, and delicacy not at all impaired, by women having it in their option to have some share in the management of public affairs.

The want of capacity for political knowledge is another objection to the granting of her civil rights to woman. But the great mass of voters do not posses, nor do they require, any very deep knowledge of political science. They are merely required to pay attention to passing events, and to be able to judge whether the candidate has ability enough to be able, and honesty enough to be willing, to attend faithfully to the interests of his constituents.*

But this is not all: woman's capacity, in this respect, has never been put to a fair test. Hitherto, when she has interfered in politics, it has not been on her own responsibility, nor with her views directed to the true and just. But it has been at the instigation of her male relatives or friends; and her efforts have been directed solely to the success of that party which they espoused. She would have thought it presumption to doubt that they were right in their opinions.

The natural character of woman, modest, diffident, retiring, made her easily yield to the dictum which pronounced her feeble and incompetent in mind as well as body; but unless her incapacity is so great as to amount to perfect irresponsibility—an opinion which few will venture to assert—her civil and legal rights must be the same as those of man. Her sex, of course, will vary them slightly; but in the main, and in principle, they ought to be the same.

The duties required by the franchise are evidently not at all inconsistent with woman's usual duties; those required by the higher office of the legislator we admit to be not so entirely consistent with the peculiar duties of women; still we deny that they are as totally opposed to these duties, as the necessary labour of many a hard-working woman or the usual pursuits of a woman of fashion. But were the duties it imposed even more directly opposed to woman's usual duties, still we should hold it to be highly pernicious to exclude women, by law, from the highest degree of political power to which individuals among that sex may aspire. We think it would be essentially unjust to restrain, by artificial barriers, those who are capable of overleaping the numberless natural ones; such women may doubtless arise at intervals; and it is for their benefit, no less than for the purpose of imparting a freer tone to the minds of women in general, that we insist on the evil nature of all these restraints. The idea of any irruption being the consequence of the

* The reader will find this argument more fully developed in a succeeding chapter.

removal of these barriers is absurd. The dread of petticoated generals, ministers and legislators, is one with which we have so little sympathy, as to have some difficulty in believing in its existence. We would have every object of ambition as open to woman as to man, perfectly secure that the natural distinctions of the sexes are quite sufficient to maintain each in its proper place, without any of those artificial restraints which man is so fond of imposing, and which only tend to shackle and debilitate those who are bound by them.

It may be urged that woman herself is well pleased with a trifling and ignoble mode of life; that levity, folly, and vanity, are so natural to the genius of her mind, that she would regard with dislike and displeasure those laborious honours which we wish to procure for her. We feel most painfully the nature and apparent force of this argument. We say *apparent* force; for, if it is found that this state of mind is a consequence of unjust institutions, with what colour can it be produced as an argument for the continuance of those institutions.

It is but too true that the greater portion of womankind are, at present, so slavish in their spirits, as to have no thought, no wish for emancipation. They have worn the shameful chain so long, as to have become insensible to the degradation. They feel not that they wear it at all, till oppression forces on them the unwelcome knowledge. This indolence and servility of mind ought not, however, to be considered inherent: it is to be attributed solely to the operation of those social arrangements of which we complain; and this very result is the most convincing proof that the principles on which they are founded are wrong. This is not the natural turn of woman's mind. It is forced on her, almost inevitably, by the opinions and prejudices which our social institutions have produced regarding her; and the sooner it can be replaced by a freer and more self-relying spirit, the better for the human race. Nothing shows the prevalence of this abject spirit more strikingly than the conduct of those women who have partially risen above it. They look around on society, and seeing that something is wrong, and that a great deal lies in the power of woman, they proclaim for her a "mission," to use all her influence in doing good, and promoting the cause of virtue; at every step, however, they protest and exclaim against the wickedness of her attempting to go so much as a hair's-breadth beyond the limits which they arbitrarily prescribe to her sphere.

Every woman—and every man, too—has, indeed, a mission, and a noble one, in the world; but in vain shall we look for zealous missionaries in those whose minds are reduced to such a wretchedly-degraded level as to be stupidly insensible to the insult of having their whole sex classed with children, malefactors, and the miserable victims of mental imbecility;

"And they, so perfect in their misery,
Not once perceive the foul disfigurement."

Missionaries must not be the willing, and almost unconscious slaves of those among whom they are sent. Their bodies may be bound, but their minds must be free and energetic. As long as woman reposes with indolent security on the reason of man, and refuses to exert her own, her mission in the world will have but little success. She must be fully enfranchised before she can either see clearly the scope of her mission, or be sufficiently aroused to engage in it. The first step in the process is to show her her shackled condition. At present, alas! she cannot even wish and strive for freedom!—she knows not that she is in any need of it. She is poor and miserable, blind and naked; and, by imagining that she is quite the reverse, loses the power she could otherwise exert of trying to improve her condition.

There are some few who have been awakened from this pleasing but ignoble dream, whose blood boils and thrills with indignant feeling at finding themselves so classed; but they are so few that, as a party, they have no name. By too many, they, and their opinions, are regarded with derision and contempt. Without putting themselves to the trouble of examining into the right or the wrong of the matter, most people smile disdainfully when the rights of woman are mentioned. Still, let not the enlightened among women be discouraged. Let me implore them to allow "the world's dread laugh" to pass by them as the idle wind which they regard not. Let them remember that a little leaven leaveneth the whole lump, and that remembrance will fortify their minds and animate their hopes. Let them remember, that the progress of opinion, though slow, is sure,—that many of those acts of public wrong-doing, which used in former days to be openly avowed and justified, would now be as openly scouted and disowned. Let them look back to the time, not very far distant, when the slavery of the whole negro race was justified as an institution of divine origin; and, when they notice the great change which has taken place in public opinion since these days, let them not despair of an equally great, or an equally speedy change, in those matters in which they are so deeply interested.

If the subject is not allowed to rest, but, on the contrary, kept before the public by constant discussion, it will soon cease to be so startling as it is at present; and truth and right will be sure to prevail in the end.

Should prejudice still, however, be too strong to allow woman all the privileges of a rational creature,—if the age is not yet far enough advanced to admit of her having a voice in legislating for herself; at least it may be loudly demanded that justice be done her as to education and the laws, these being the results for which powers of legislation are most desirable. Let very shame induce those who legislate for her to be quite sure that the laws enforced with regard to her are just and right. Let all that are obnoxious be repealed. Let all that are necessary for her better protection be speedily enacted. Let those who interest themselves in schemes of education, no longer show themselves so shallow as to pass over the education of woman in silent contempt. Let all the grants of money for educational purposes be fairly divided for the benefit of both sexes. Although not very well fitted to battle for her rights in the first instance, let her but once get fair play and she will soon show herself worthy of it. The true interest of every individual, as well as of every class of human beings, is so closely bound up in that of the race, that if man will but be prevailed on to act with true generosity to woman, he shall soon find that generosity redound to his own advantage.

CHAPTER VII.

OBJECTIONS IN "WOMAN'S RIGHT AND DUTIES" EXAMINED.

"Not rash equality, but equal rights." — *Byron.*

Having thus briefly considered the subject in the manner suggested by our own mind, we propose, in the next place, to examine the arguments brought forward in "Woman's Rights and Duties," and in an article in *The Edinburgh Review*, which notices this work and some others of the same class.

"Woman's Rights and Duties" is written by a woman, and is a work of considerable research. The great tendency of it seems to favour the opinions we have expressed; yet the writer arrives at a contrary conclusion. In the body of her work she takes but little notice of woman's having any claim to political privileges, defining the extent of her rights to be a "right to all the self-government which can be left her, without deranging man's purposes or man's enjoyments." When she does notice woman's claim to more extended rights, it is but to reject it. The ground on which she justifies this proceeding is, that equality is an impossible state of society which, were it to have place to-day, would be destroyed to-morrow. And that, were it possible, it is not just; that it is both right and reasonable that the strongest of mind and body should have supremacy over the weaker; that the exercise of this supremacy will be for the good of all, and is justifiable on that ground alone.

As to the first of these opinions, we join her most cordially in thinking perfect equality an absurd and visionary scheme: not so, however, do we think of equal civil rights. Perfect equality and equal civil rights are two very different things; the reader will find the assumption, that they are one and the same, discussed more fully in the following chapter. Perfect equality is an absurdity incapable of realization. Equal political rights is a wise and sober theory, every way capable of being put in practice; and which, if it be visionary at all, is rendered so not from any innate inapplicability, but by the obtuseness and perverseness of men who, wedded to old customs good in their day, will listen to no arguments against them, now that that day is gone by.

Again we agree with our author, that subordination is due from woman to man; but we also think that her possession of equal civil rights is quite consistent with this subordination, and is the best guarantee that man's supremacy will not be abused. An equalization of civil rights most certainly is necessary for justice; but it does not thence follow that an equalization of *all* rights is required. This admission demands explanation. We mean, then, that a rich man may justly claim a right to property, which a poor man has no just right to claim: so far their rights are unequal. This rich man may be imprudent and foolish, while the poor man may be wise and provident: again their rights are unequal; the one is entitled to an honour and respect to which the other has no claim. All these, and a thousand other inequalities of condition, may, and will exist, even were the political privileges of all completely equal. As a proof of this, we may see that they really do exist even amongst those who are now equal in political privileges. Insubordination and confusion are not, then, necessary results of civil equality amongst those who are equals now; and we see no reason to fear this result in the case of women more than others.

These opinions—first, that it is folly to attempt forcing perfect equality; and second, that man is entitled to supremacy over woman, in both of which we agree with our author—form her ground for entirely dismissing the subject of woman's political rights from the body of her work; but, in a note which we propose to annex, she gives more particular reasons for thinking that woman ought not to have the right of voting.*

The first reason is, that women are all under influence, and therefore incapable of voting. For our part we go even farther than our author, and are quite of opinion that this is one of those rules to which there is no exception; but if women are thereby incapable of voting, so also must all men. We believe it will be allowed, that not only all womankind, but the

* "A question has occasionally been raised, and I believe by more than one writer, whether the right of voting be not unjustly withheld from women. But it seems an almost conclusive objection to giving them the franchise, that by the very principle upon which it is bestowed, women are unfit for it, being always under influence. There are no doubt some cases of exception to that rule, but so there are to every other rule, by which persons are excluded from that right. Perhaps no other rule is so extensively true, as that women are under influence. But, further, women have no political interests apart from men. The public measures that are taken, the restrictions or taxes imposed on the community, do not affect them more than male subjects. In all such respects the interests of the two sexes are identified. As citizens, therefore, they are sufficiently represented already. To give them the franchise would just double the number of voters, without introducing any new interest; and, far from improving society, few things would tend more to dissever and corrupt it.

44

whole race of man is under influence. Where is the single human being that can be said to act solely from the dictates of his own mind, totally uninfluenced by any being or circumstance outer to himself? Such a one is not to be found.

>——"Men's judgments are
>A parcel of their fortunes: and things outward
>Do draw the inward quality after them."

Accordingly, we consider that, by this writer's mode of reasoning, neither sex can be qualified to vote, each being under influence to the other. We cannot deny that woman is under influence; but we assert that this is no objection whatever, man being also under influence. If the one sex is to be excluded on that account, the other ought to be so also.

But the truth of the matter is, that it is not simply being under influence which constitutes a good ground of objection against any one as a voter, else all would be excluded, but it is being under *undue* influence: which phrase we have always understood to mean a small degree of bribery; not exactly the barefaced sale of a vote, but rather the barter of it,—the giving it for some consideration of personal advantage. This, however, is not likely to be her meaning, for she has made woman's greater liability to political corruption a distinct argument, which we shall examine in its turn, for her exclusion from this privilege; and as to the general charge of being under influence, it is of no force whatever as a reason for depriving any one of the right of voting. But is not this a very curious turn that affairs now take? One moment we are told, that woman must do everything by her influence; the next, that she is so overpowered by the superior influence of man, that she is incapable of holding or expressing an independent opinion!

This writer's second reason for approving the exclusion of woman from the right of voting is, that women, having no political interests, apart from men, and taxes not affecting them more than men, they are already virtually represented; and so, of course, to give them the

"But disabilities or oppressions, to which they are subject *as women*, could not be in any degree remedied by possessing the franchise. Interests of that description, being exclusively female, would come into collision, not, as in other cases, with the interests of a class or party, but with those of the whole male sex, and one of two things would happen. Either one sex would be arrayed in a sort of general hostility to the other, or they would be divided amongst themselves. Than the first, nothing could possibly be devised more disastrous to the condition of women. They would be utterly crushed; the old prejudices would be revived against their education, or their meddling with anything but household duties. Every man of mature age would probably stipulate, on marrying, that his wife should forswear the use of the franchise, and all ideas connected with political influence, or the coarse and degrading contentions of the elections.

"If each sex were divided among themselves on particular questions, unprincipled men would franchise would be but to double the number of voters without introducing any new interest. This is but a paltry excuse for depriving a half of the species of the rights of rational and responsible creatures. The same pretence might be used, with equal plausibility, for disfranchising every third or fourth of the present voters; for the political interests of the mass of men are the same, and it would certainly save a little trouble were the number of voters reduced.

Her third argument is, that the disabilities or oppressions to which they are liable as women could not so be remedied. Interests of that kind, being exclusively female, would come into collision, not, as in other cases, with a party, but with the whole male sex. This, truly, is a fine account of the protection and gallantry which woman is to look for at the hands of man! Observe here, that the cause of collision is not represented to be any opposition to male interests, it is simply that the interests advocated are exclusively female. Being exclusively for the interest of woman, is said to be a sufficient reason for rousing the opposition of the whole male sex to any measures! If this be true, there is no need of looking for difficulties beyond woman's acquisition of the franchise; for nothing which can be demanded on behalf of woman is more for her exclusive benefit than the acquisition of this right; and if it rouses the opposition of the whole male sex, she never can acquire it. Do we then despair of her obtaining this right? Very far from it. How often do we see a very small party, because they have got the right side of a question, oblige a very large and powerful party continually to give way

endeavour to secure their elections by creating female parties. Men of such characters now disguise their personal interests, by affecting to adopt some measure popular with the mob, or suited only to the partial interests of some locality. They do not always desire to forward such measures; but they delude and corrupt the people by using them as pretexts. If women had the franchise, men would address themselves to the worst part of the sex, the most clamorous, and those least restrained by female decorum. The pretexts made use of to delude them would probably be injudicious, as measures, and condemned by the informed and reflecting of their own sex.

"It has been maintained through this work, that the interests of women can be served chiefly through opinion, though without denying that some legal enactments might also be required for certain special hardships. Can it be seriously imagined, by any dispassionate woman, that these legal changes could be as well brought about by the power of now and then forcing an advocate into the legislature, as by their general influence in society, won through their own moral and mental deserts, and identified in men's minds with the influence which justice must always retain over their feelings?

"Conducted as elections now are, scenes of violence and tumult, women would be subject to every species of insult. It may be imagined that a remedy might be found for that; but what remedy would be found for inflictions no law could reach or define, and which they would suffer at home for that exertion of their right, which was opposed to the interests or prejudices of their male relations? Can it be supposed the Ballot would be any security? Surely not. Intimidation and bribery, already so mischievous, would be far more dangerous to the timidity and comparative poverty of women, than they now are to men. And, educated as they are, their most honest decisions would be worse formed, even than those of the other sex, defective as the political knowledge of the greater number is still allowed to be." — *Woman's Rights and Duties.*

before them, till at last it is acknowledged on all hands, that without even striking a blow they have gained a victory. We shall only mention one instance of this kind. By what a small and apparently insignificant party was the agitation for the abolition of the slave-trade begun about fifty years ago? And see what it has now accomplished, with no arms save truth and justice! Not only the abolition of the slave-trade by Britain, but the total extinction of slavery in all her colonies; and, more lately, the coalition of the most powerful European nations to put a stop to the shocking traffic.

This persuasive power which a truth once started seems to possess of insinuating itself, silently and almost imperceptibly, into the tone of society, shows also, very clearly, how, should woman come to be represented, she need not fear any angry or jealous opposition to those measures which are required for the ameliorating of her condition. Even if she have a very small number of representatives in her interest, still they will be enough to obtain a hearing; and though man's immediate and selfish interests may cause much opposition, yet, if the measures be really just, we have little doubt of the result.

Not but what we allow, at once, that the vulgar, short-sighted, immediate interests of man are opposed to the true interests of woman; but we contend that it is these low and narrow views of his interest which alone require to be combated in man. That there is a danger, or rather a certainty of opposition from these, is rather an argument in favour of representation than against it; for, if being represented, the interests of woman are sure to come into collision with the most generally obvious interests of the other sex,—how much more, not being represented, must her interests be entirely lost sight of and forgotten. How far man, in his general practice, is from looking beyond to-day and himself, to the interests of future years and the race of man, is evident enough; and our author freely grants it, in assuming that he will oppose everything that is exclusively for the interest of woman. Hence one great use of representation to woman,—her cause is heard, and the subtle and overpowering influence of opinion begins silently to work in her favour. Nor would this tendency of individuals to attend solely to their own immediate interests work against the wellbeing of society, had every one equal political privileges; for then wealth, knowledge, and natural intelligence, would exercise only their legitimate influence on society, and every interest would have its due value in the competition. Were it the case that man looked to his own and woman's true interests in a wide and extensive sense, we have little doubt that they would be found to be ultimately the same; and then, of course, representation would be less necessary for woman, though we think that even then it would be required for her independence and moral dignity.

It will be seen, then, that while conscious of the jealous opposition to the rights and interests of woman which may be, for a length of time, expected from man, we are not blind to the less obvious truth, that the real interest of man and woman must ever be the same. We believe it will be allowed, that there is not a single interest of woman, of which it can be said with truth, that to do her justice in that respect would be to inflict a real injury on man. Let us, for instance, look for an instant to the unjust laws which have force with regard to woman. It may seem, at first sight, that the abolition of these is the exclusive interest of woman; but let any intelligent person say, whether it is not almost equally the interest of mankind and womankind that they should be repealed. Is it for the interest of man that he may tyrannize over his female relatives with impunity? Certainly not. Even less for his interest than for that of his unfortunate victims; for they may exercise forbearance and charity towards him who oppresses them, and so constantly go on improving themselves; while he, by the very exercise of oppression, deteriorates his own mind, and thus, in a manner, loses the chief end—to himself—of his existence, namely the gradual improvement of his nature.

Allowing, however, that women have some interests which are strictly and exclusively female, it by no means follows that these must necessarily be opposed to the true interests of man. We trust that the interests of woman merely require to be discussed and advocated; and that, when this is fairly done, it will be seen by both sexes that their respective interests, even those most exclusively male and female, do not at all interfere with each other.

Allowing, for the sake of argument, that such a thing were possible, as that some question might arise in which the interests of the sexes must be diametrically opposed to each other,—if what was justice to the one could not but be injustice to the other, then woman must at once give way. Nay, such is the nobleness and generosity of her nature, that we believe, in such an almost inconceivable case, woman never would stand up for herself. Were she forced to choose, she would much rather, we believe, suffer a wrong than inflict one.

Such a state of things, however, is happily beyond the range of possibility. Affairs are better arranged for us than we arrange them for ourselves. It is incredible that, in any state of society, justice to one class can be done *only* at the expense of injustice to another. In such a case, tossing up would be the fairest mode of deciding the hostile interests.

Another objection is, that those who now flatter the mob, for factious purposes, would then flatter the women. What unprincipled men might do, or how far they might succeed, is hard to say; we will only observe, that we consider women, in general, as good judges of character as men: both, of course, being liable to be imposed on for a time, by a plausible exterior. We must say, we see but little force in this objection, as an argument for doing woman the great wrong of depriving her of her just rights, to secure her the small good of freeing her from the flattery which would seek to delude her into injudicious measures; measures which, if really injudicious, would certainly be but temporary.

We quite agree with the writer of "Woman's Rights and Duties," that it is principally through opinion that the condition of woman can be improved. But should public opinion so far change as to allow of her claims to equal rights, we are quite at a loss to conceive why it should be apprehended, that a consequence of those rights being acknowledged would be a "loss of their general influence on society, won by their own moral and mental deserts." If for the purpose of obtaining those legal enactments which are most necessary for ameliorating the condition of woman, there was absolutely no alternative but using the power of now and then forcing an advocate into the legislature, or woman's general influence on society, we dare say every woman, whether dispassionate or otherwise, would prefer the latter method. We hope, however, we may be allowed, without laying ourselves open to the charge of any unreasonable passion, to pause for a moment, that we may see clearly whether we are required to make this choice.

Our authoress here contrasts woman's general influence on society, with the power of now and then *forcing*—as she calls it—some few advocates into the legislature. But woman's rights rest altogether on reason and justice, and sink without resistance before the first appearance of force. Never, then, can it be said that she has *forced* advocates into the legislature. No: it is her moral influence on society which must win, not force, her rights; and dispassionate people would be very apt to think, that the fact of her being represented in the legislature would add weight to her general influence rather than destroy it; since it is by that very influence, not by forcible intrusion, that she must obtain that privilege. We can see no reason whatever for her influence and her representation being contrasted with each other, as if the one was necessarily incompatible with the other. If, by her influence, she gains representation, her representation will certainly react and increase her influence instead of destroying it.

The tumults which often take place at elections are but a paltry reason, and our authoress does well to reject that argument; these being things which, she says truly, ought themselves to be reformed—and, indeed, they have been greatly amended, and are in process of being still more so; of course, then, they cannot be made use of as an argument in this case.

We cannot at all assent to the somewhat gratuitous assertion, that women would be more open to intimidation and bribery than men. The ground on which this charge is made, is the comparative poverty and timidity of woman. Is it then proved that a person's honesty (putting him above absolute want) depends upon his riches or poverty? Are the richest classes of people least politically corrupt? Or are they not the most so? Has bribery not decreased since the late extension of the franchise? And will not the almost impossibility of bribery, when the franchise is still farther extended, be an ample atonement for any additional trouble (one of the chief reasons of this writer for withholding the franchise from woman) which even a double extension of the constituency will produce. As to intimidation, there is nothing in which those writers who have studied the characteristics of the sexes agree in more, than the opinion, that woman excels man in passive courage. And it is this, more than active bravery, which is required to withstand intimidation. Indeed, we believe, that if any distinction were to be made in this matter, it would rather prove the reverse; for the moral perception of woman, like her physical organisation, is more delicate than that of man, and her power of endurance, at least, equal to his. However short may be the page of history devoted to woman, there remains enough to show, that for conscience' sake she can endure with as much constancy as the noblest of men.

Even if it were quite clear that women were more liable to become corrupt—in a political sense—than men, that is nothing to the purpose. If any class—say bakers—had been proved, beyond a doubt, to be the most corrupt voters in her majesty's dominions, would that have been a good reason for depriving all bakers of the franchise? Most certainly not. The individuals who were proved guilty are those alone who ought to be punished, not the class to which they belong; much less would the mere suspicion, that a certain class was more likely to become corrupt than others, prove a sufficient reason for its disfranchisement. If it were an established rule, that the most corrupt *class* was instantly to be disfranchised, there would very soon be no freemen left; for as their is no class without some corrupt members, so one class after another, beginning with that which was most corrupt, would be liable to suffer this penalty.

The occasion it might furnish for domestic dissension, is, with our authoress, another reason for withholding their civil rights from women. I must here again remind my readers, that it is easy to imagine ill consequences following in the train of almost any change. If, however, the change be from oppression to justice, from wrong to right, we ought not, most certainly, to allow the apprehensions of the timid, as to the result, to interfere with our judgment. No evil which it may be supposed will follow the granting of certain rights, can be taken as an impugnment of those rights. Do not evil that good may come, is a precept that, without any violence, may be extended to, Do not continue doing evil for fear of some new evil following the putting away of the first evil. There is not, however, much to be apprehended on this score. The objection is plausible, but ceases to be very formidable on a nearer inspection. Increased care would then be taken to connect ourselves only with those whose sentiments were similar to our own, or, at least, so far congenial that, though differing in details, we could entirely sympathize in principle; and this increased care would, we think, be favourable rather than otherwise to domestic happiness. When a man found that society recognised a reasonable and responsible creature in his sister, wife, or daughter, he would no longer be filled with indignation when he found some difference of opinion between any of those relatives and himself.

The submission which is naturally and properly due from woman to man, is quite consistent with equal rights; and the equality of those rights is the only guarantee that more than that due submission shall not be exacted by man. With these sentiments, and those we have expressed all along in this book, we can feel but small alarm for the dissension in families, which it is apprehended equality of civil rights between male and female would be apt to produce. It would only induce people to be more careful in choosing partners of a congenial mind; which would rather lessen domestic dissension than introduce more of it. A man would not then be obliged so frequently as he now is, to look abroad for a friend to sympathize with him in the interest which he takes in public affairs. Instead of a mere upper servant, a woman would then be a companion and friend to her husband.

Then, after all, we hear some one exclaim, All the advantage you would derive would be the inconvenience of double the number of voters. But we answer, No, indeed, that is not all; for we gain many advantages: among others, independence and dignity of mind for half of mankind; and where is the propriety of paying such a price, as the forfeiture of these, for the avoidance of so paltry an inconvenience? To abase all womankind in their own eyes is rather too high a price to pay for saving a little trouble.

Our authoress gives the present education of woman as another reason for withholding civil equality. But this is a mockery: if the education be wrong let it be amended. At the very utmost, this can only be a reason for deferring the grant of their rights, not for extinguishing them altogether. And we should fancy there is but small danger of their civil and legal equality being acknowledged so speedily, but that before then some alterations may be introduced into the usual flimsy style of female education. Indeed, if the agitation of this question should lead to no other result, we hope it will at least be useful in obtaining for woman the advantage of a more substantial education.

These are all the arguments which induce our authoress to withhold her suffrage from her sex: to her mind they have been sufficient; to ours they have had but little force. It appears to us—and we hope we have proved this to the satisfaction of the reader—that what she argues against is justice, and that her arguments do not even tend to show that it is not justice, but are merely opinions, that it would be inexpedient to do justice.

CHAPTER VIII.

EXAMINATION OF AN ARTICLE IN "THE EDINBURGH REVIEW."

"Preferring sense, from chin that's bare,
To nonsense throned in whisker'd hair."—*Green.*

The work of which we spoke in the last chapter, "Woman's Rights and Duties," is noticed very favourably in an article in *The Edinburgh Review* for April–July, 1841; and I now propose to examine some of the arguments and opinions which the reviewer himself brings forward, in the course of his remarks on this and similar publications. His great objections to woman's having political rights are, first, her inferiority in mental power; and second, the disorder which would then have place instead of the present comfortable arrangements of domestic life. With respect to the first objection, we think the readers will be very few who will not agree with us, that there is no such inherent feebleness in the mind of woman, taken as a class, as necessarily to preclude her from exercising the elective franchise with deliberation and propriety. Nay, we believe that it will generally be allowed, that the superior classes of British women are more capable—as far as mere capacity is concerned—of exercising those rights, than the lower classes of the present electors. In fact, the usual duties of woman—as we have faintly attempted to shadow them forth in our comparison of these duties with those of man—require infinitely more capacity and intelligence than the exercise of this simplest of political rights. Indeed, this is the only writer we have seen who does not disclaim the idea of incapacity as a reason for withholding political rights from woman. Jeremy Bentham declares the test of intellectual aptitude for the discharge of the duties attached to this right, to apply equally to man and woman; and Charles Fox, who was in favour of that scheme of reform which would bring forward the greatest number of independent voters, rests the exclusion of woman simply upon her being in a dependent position, disclaiming, most distinctly, the idea of any inherent incapacity. The second objection of this writer, namely, the domestic disorder which would ensue, he has never even attempted to make good, as we shall show, after having more

53

fully discussed his first objection, which we shall now present to the reader in his own words.

"It may be plausibly urged, that as the rightful course of civilisation tends to raise woman to the level of man, it will, or ought to end in establishing the equality of the sexes in power and influence upon the affairs of the world; and that everything short of this equality is a wrongful contravention of the ultimate designs of providence. This mode of reasoning is plausible, but unsound. Civilisation ameliorates the condition of woman, because it lessens the influence of physical strength in proportion to that of mind; and because woman is more nearly equal to man in power of intellect than in strength of limb. But it does not thence follow, that in mental faculties she is equal, or that the height to which her position may be raised by the advance of civilisation may not have its limits far short of complete equality."

For our part, we have no doubt that this is all very true; but, at the same time, our position—that woman has a right to representation—is not at all affected by it. We agree at once, that woman falls short of the mental vigour of man; and we have but little doubt—although we confess we have a little—that this deficiency is inherent in her nature; and, if so, absolute and complete equality is out of the question. But equality of civil rights is not complete equality.

We have always understood, that the equalization of the rights of *men* was principally useful for preventing the strong—whether of body or mind—from oppressing the weak. We, in our blindness, cannot see, in the acknowledged weakness of a class, any reason for taking away the civil rights of its members; but, at the same time, neither can we see that granting civil equality to that class can raise it to complete equality with another class, possessed, indeed, of no more than equal civil privileges, but endowed at the same time with a double portion of intellectual vigour. The rights of woman, happily, are not founded upon the supposition of her perfect equality with man; they are founded on the acknowledged fact, that she is a rational being, responsible for her actions both to God and man, and, therefore, having a right to a voice in the making of those laws which are to govern her actions. The reader will see this more fully discussed in the first chapter devoted to the Rights of Woman.

The reviewer now goes into a lengthened discussion, to prove that woman is not equal to man in her mental faculties. The ground which we take renders it unnecessary that we should follow him closely here, though we intend to examine the fairness and soundness of his arguments on this point when we come to speak of female education.

Yet, before leaving the subject of the mental inequality of the sexes, we cannot resist giving one more quotation. After estimating the comparative merits of male and female painters, poets, and musical composers, and of course giving the palm to man, he goes on:—

"To turn from the ornamental arts to institute a comparison respecting the exercise of intellect on those important public matters on which depend the welfare of a state, might seem almost futile and absurd. Yet we cannot dismiss the comparison altogether in silence, while there are those who seriously, and, we will add, plausibly, hold that women should be admitted to a share in the exercise of political power. To such advocates many might deem it a sufficient answer to ask, What evidence of the possession of legislative and administrative abilities has been hitherto given by woman? Debarred as she is from the practice of politics, what proof has she given of consummate knowledge of them in theory? What work has issued from a female hand, what words have fallen from female lips, fraught with such lessons of political wisdom as man might study with advantage?"

We confess that it is with great satisfaction that we see the advocates of the continuance of female depression reduced to use such miserable arguments as these in support of their cause. By his own showing, the previous position of woman—"debarred from the practice of politics,"—renders it next to impossible that she should have done what this writer requires of her. Surely the very circumstance of her being so debarred would have the effect of turning her thoughts entirely from the subject, and so of course prevent her from showing any turn for theoretical speculations on it.

In the very same volume of *The Edinburgh Review* which contains this article, is an account of the Port-Royalists, and the noble struggle which they maintained against the Jesuits in the reign of Louis XIV. Two ladies—cousins, and of the house of Arnauld—who successively held the office of abbess, are no less remarkable for the virtues than the genius and learning they possess. Of the first of these noble ladies it is said, that while exiled from her convent by the persecutions of the Jesuits, and sinking into the grave under the most fearful bodily and mental sufferings, she dictated, at each momentary remission of her agonies, a letter, long and justly celebrated as a model of epistolary correspondence. "It has no trace of debility, still less of resentment. Her defence is as clear and as collected as if, in the fulness of health, she had been conducting the cause of another." Of the second lady it is said, "If she was the writer of the memoir in defence of her monastery, which

bears her name"—*and there is not the slightest reason for doubting this*—
"there was no apparent obstacle but her sex and her profession to her
successful rivalry of the greatest masters of judicial eloquence in
France." We see, then, how much opportunity of development may do
for the intellect of woman. These old and feeble women, recluses from
the world, required only to be called upon, to show publicly that clear
and calm reasoning, that strong but graceful eloquence, which could not
be surpassed by the first advocates of France. And who can tell how
many women there have been in whom talents such as these have
slumbered, or been exerted on matters too small to attract any public
notice?

In return for all these questions, we shall only ask this writer, whether
he knows it for a fact, that the ten-pound voters were obliged, previous
to receiving the franchise, to prove before a select committee, that some
of the members of their body had enlightened the world by such lessons
of political wisdom as he describes? And if one of them must be such a
paragon, why must not each one of them? Why should a single soul be
allowed political privileges, who has not satisfactorily proved that he is a
treasure of legislative and deliberative wisdom?

For our part, we should think that even when the constituency was
much more limited than it is at present, any such evidence of the
possession of deliberative and administrative abilities by the voters was
not thought necessary, and would have been looked for in vain. Indeed,
the possession of such abilities is not at all required by the nature of their
duties, which are such as any person of ordinary sense and intelligence
is quite able to perform with propriety. It is not to be expected that the
great majority of the constituency can make themselves acquainted with
the merits of those intricate questions, the consideration of which will
occupy their representatives; want of time, even did they possess the
necessary capacity, renders this impossible with the great mass even of
the present voters. All that is required of a constituent is to have
sufficient intelligence to judge correctly, whether the candidate has
ability enough to be able, and honesty enough to be willing, to represent
his interests judiciously and faithfully.

An apt illustration of this point may be had in the subject of negro
slavery. It has been said that negroes are an inferior race of men, with
fully as much appearance of truth as that women generally are inferior
to men; and yet what sort of moralist would he now be considered, who
would propose on that account to continue the iniquitous institution of
slavery? And again, who is so blind as not to see, that if they really are an

inferior order of men, no equality of civil rights can raise them to complete equality with the more favoured of their race?

Complete equality of civil rights is often very erroneously spoken of, as if it were an attempt to force an absolute equality in all things. The writer of "Woman's Rights and Duties" especially, takes this for granted, and goes into a laboured discussion to prove that such a state of society could not continue. For our part, we require no argument, but a mere statement of the case, to prove to us that such a state of things could not be established even for an instant. It is neither expected nor desired—even were it possible—that civil equality should raise the foolish, the ignorant, the weak, and the poor, to the same level as the wise, the learned, the strong, and the rich. All that the advocates of equality of rights assert is, that the wise and rich, owing to the very circumstance of their wisdom or riches—prudence, perseverance, anything, in short, which raises them above the mass—exert naturally the legitimate influence over society which their superiority in these respects ought to give them, and that there is no need of conferring extra rights and privileges on particular classes at the expense of the less-favoured portion of men. If any barriers are necessary at all, they are more required to prevent the powerful—in whatever their strength consists—from oppressing and tyrannizing over their inferiors—in whatever that inferiority consists—than to prevent those inferiors raising themselves, or pulling down their superiors, till they all stand on the same level. All history vouches for the truth of this opinion; for is it not full of the tyranny of the distinguished few over the great mass of men?

We shall now examine the second and last objection of the reviewer, and begin by presenting it to the reader in his own words. "The advocates for woman's participation with man in those political functions which are now exclusively his, would, after all, gain but little in support of their theory, if they could prove that there exists in woman an equality of intellectual power, an equal aptitude for political affairs and the more important and serious business of public life. Grant all this; yet the participation of woman (not in individual cases, but as part of a general system) could not be admitted without infringing upon that important law which prescribes a division of duties as one of the most important elements in the conduct and transaction of human affairs. Take an instance (and there are probably many) in which the wife has an equal capacity with her husband for that business which falls naturally to his lot, and would be able to take his place and transact his affairs quite as well as himself;—assume, next, that the husband has an equal aptitude for all those domestic duties which are assigned by custom to the wife; yet, can any one doubt, that if each, during alternate periods, were to assume the duties of the other, that the result would be, that the whole duties, public and domestic, thus divided among them, would be less efficiently performed than if each adhered exclusively to his own department?"

The first sentence in this paragraph contains an assertion which, we suppose, the second is meant to illustrate or prove. Now, in the first place, we deny the truth of the assertion; and, in the second, contend that the intended illustration or proof is so entirely foreign to the point in dispute, that we cannot imagine how it could be mistaken for an illustration or proof of it. The assertion is, that woman's participation in political power would be an infringement of the law which prescribes a division of duties; but it might as well be said that the participation in political power of a baker, a smith, or a shoemaker, is an infringement of that law. The truth seems to be, that although there is such a division of those minor duties which belong rather to the situation of the individual than to the human being absolutely, yet that this law is totally inapplicable to the greatest and most important duties of mankind, which are equally incumbent on all. For instance, it is the duty of the baker to bake his bread, of the smith to hammer his iron, of the shoemaker to make his shoes; and it would be an infringement of the law which prescribes a division of duties, were they to undertake these occupations of each other alternately. But there are many duties, which it is no infringement of this law, that each of them alike is called on to perform,—among others, that of voting for a representative. The law of the division of labour is strictly applicable only to the duties attendant upon the occupation of the individual; there is no division of those duties which every one owes to his neighbour, his country, and his race. This law does not prescribe that each person have only one duty to perform; it does not require that one man confine his endeavours to be honest, another to be patriotic, and another to be philanthropic, but only, that he must not pretend to undertake the duties of a number of different professions or occupations. According to this writer's view of a division of duties, respresentation would cease, and the duty of voting would be confined, even amongst men, to a select few, who would have nothing else to do but to vote! According to our view of this law, we think a woman could perform all her present duties quite consistently with the performance of the additional one of voting for a representative.

We trust our readers will now see that this argument derives its apparent force from the confusion in which the writer has involved the duties of business—in which this division is useful and necessary—with the common duties of humanity, all of which are equally incumbent upon each individual.

What is produced in the second sentence, as a proof or illustration of the assertion in the first, is neither more nor less than another assertion, (and one which we dare say nobody will deny the truth of, at least who is acquainted with the old ballad of the Wife of Auchtermuchty,) namely, that a very uncomfortable state of affairs would be the result, were men and women to perform each other's duties alternately! But who ever proposed that they should do so? And would this be a necessary consequence of a woman's having a vote? What has the exercise by her of political privileges to do with her undertaking to perform alternately her husband's business duties and her own domestic ones? But, above all, what has this whole view of the case to do among the arguments of a writer who scouts entirely the idea of a woman who has a husband having also a vote, and strictly confines his consideration of the subject to the case of old maids and widows?

For our own part, we are unfortunately so obtuse as to find it very difficult to imagine such a state of things as that supposed by this writer. The domestic duties which *custom* has assigned to the wife, the husband might, perhaps, perform; but those which *nature* has assigned her, he would find it rather difficult to manage. The reviewer has given no reason whatever for supposing, that the bestowing of civil rights on woman would at all interfere with the present arrangement—by which the rearing of the children and the superintendence of the household economy is given to the wife, and the care of bringing in the supplies is left to the husband; and we fancy, that the time requisite for voting conscientiously, will be found to interfere as little with the ordinary occupations of woman as it does with the business duties of man. We believe that, whatever may be done to improve the social position of woman, nature and custom will always continue to go hand in hand, in preserving in its prominent points—of domestic affairs to woman, and business affairs to man—the arrangements which at present prevail.

The reader will do well to notice the ambiguity and confusion of ideas which pervades the last quotation we have made, and the dexterity of the writer in sliding off entirely from the point at issue into another subject so near akin to it, that the change may escape the notice of an inattentive or hurried reader; and yet so distinct from it, that the instant the attention is arrested, one sees that there is very little connexion between the points. The pretension of the first sentence in this passage is, that the writer is about to prove that woman's participation of political functions would infringe upon the law which prescribes a division of duties, into domestic for woman, and business for man. But how does the second perform the promise of the first? Why, by leaving the point entirely,—and, I may add, it is never recurred to; for, in the last sentence, the writer glides, without any apparent consciousness of the change, into the more easy task of showing how uncomfortable a state of things would be produced were the sexes to perform all each other's duties alternately. What! is it then impossible for a woman to vote for a representative without going every alternate day or week to her husband or brother's office, he, meanwhile, performing her duties at home!

These, then, are the only objections this writer has to produce against the claim of woman to civil rights. The first, woman's intellectual inferiority to man, we hold to be no argument at all; unless that inferiority be so marked and proved as to do away with the impression which has hitherto prevailed, that woman is a rational, moral, and accountable creature. The inferiority, to have any weight, must amount to a greater difference than exists between the most intellectual and the most stupid of men; for no man has his civil rights taken from him on account of inferior ability, unless his incapacity amounts to mental imbecility.

The last objection, that it would be an infringement of the division of duties, is entitled to still less weight than the first; since we have shown that the writer himself either attaches so little importance to it, or is so unable to maintain his position, that he immediately deserts it. If it be an argument at all, it must be evident that it can apply only to the case of married women; yet a few pages after, when speaking more particularly of the right of voting for a representative in parliament, we find our reviewer saying—

"In thus replying to the foregoing arguments, we assume that it is never contemplated that the right of voting should be claimed by married women during their husbands' lives; or for unmarried women living under the protection of their parents."

After stating these two objections, the reviewer goes on to notice and—according to his own notions—refute certain arguments which have been brought forward by those of our opinion. We shall allow him both to produce the difficulty urged by his opponents, and attempt to solve it in his own words. He says—

"It is urged that we cannot consistently plead for the exclusion of women from all political functions, while, by a provision of our constitution, which experience teaches us to regard with peculiar approbation and respect, the highest political functions may be exercised by a woman." The reviewer's answer is:—"The fact that these kingdoms can be ruled over by a queen, may be an effectual answer to an argument in favour of the exclusion of women from all exercise of political power; but the absence of analogy between the position and functions of the sovereign and those of any of her subjects, prevents the example from being applicable in support of any other case. If it could be applied in any case, the least remote in point of analogy would be that of peeresses in their own right; and the privilege claimed for them would be, that they should sit and vote in the House of Lords. But if any advocate of female rights has ever seriously proposed that they should mingle among men in the stormy debates of a deliberative assembly, he will be considered, we think, by a vast majority even among women, as scarcely entitled to a serious reply."

Let it be borne in mind, that the great and almost the only objection which this writer makes to granting political privileges to women is, their inferior mental capacity, and the unreasonableness of this line of argument will appear in all its rich absurdity. Is it then true that royalty is such a political farce, that its functions may, with perfect safety to the state, be exercised by one of a sex whose mental incapacity is the chief reason for withholding the lowest political privilege from its members? If royalty be not such a complete farce—as we believe it is not—the peculiar approbation and respect of this writer for that provision of our constitution which consigns the highest power in the state to such incapable hands, is certainly one of those things which are extremely difficult to be accounted for.

Between the position and functions of an absolute sovereign and any of her subjects, there is, of course, no analogy. But we do not at all see this to be the case with regard to the sovereign of this country, and any of her subjects who exercise political rights. If the sovereign of these realms really possesses that power and performs those functions which in theory she is supposed to do, then we can see only a difference in degree and in complexity, but none whatever in the intrinsic nature of the duties performed by her and those performed by that portion of her subjects who exercise political functions of a lower order. The queen is a whole branch of the legislature in her own person; the voter is but the fraction of a fraction. The queen has the power of creating as many legislators as she pleases, the power of legislating remains in whose families for ever: the voter has merely a voice in investing with the legislative power a single individual, and that temporarily. There certainly is some analogy between these functions of a sovereign and a voter; the difference being, that those of a sovereign are by much the most complex and difficult of performance. But, according to this writer, the various and complicated duties of a ruler are capable of being effectively performed by a woman; and, at the same time, a woman's limited capacity is an insuperable barrier to her performance of the simple duty of a voter for a representative. Such is the careless and inconsequential line of argument pursued by a writer who decides on woman's inferior capacity for close logical reasoning! Even should a woman be the writer of this article, however, we would not hold that to be conclusive against the whole sex.

Should we allow that the theoretical functions of royalty are practically exercised not by the queen but by her ministers, then the most important duty of our sovereign would be the choice of wise and energetic ministers to represent her. Now, surely this bears no such remote analogy to the duty of voting for a representative in parliament; and we should most certainly conclude, that the mischief done by incapacity in the first instance, would be infinitely greater than by incapacity in the second.

We deny, then, that there is an absence of analogy between the functions of subject and sovereign. This is true only where the sovereignty is absolute. Whenever the subject is allowed any share in the legislature, the nature of the functions he performs will be found to bear a very considerable resemblance to those exercised by the sovereign. Putting, however, the point of analogy entirely aside, and allowing, for argument's sake, that though women may be too great fools—for it must be remembered that want of capacity is with this writer the great objection to woman's rights—to be entrusted with a voice in the choosing of a single legislator, yet that still they are possessed of sufficient ability to be the rulers of kingdoms. I say, letting these apparent contradictions pass, let us see whether we can find anything so utterly absurd in the idea of a peeress in her own right sitting and voting in the House of Lords. It is evident that the idea in itself is not absurd, but is merely made so by the customs of this country, which do not allow of it. It is not, for instance, more absurd than the idea of the queen presiding and taking part in the debates in her privy-council. This, doubtless, would seem very absurd to the inhabitants of other countries, who have not been familiarized with the idea of a woman maintaining the position and performing the duties of a ruler. The foreigner smiles at the idea of a reigning queen, because he is unaccustomed to it; it seems to his mind odd and strange. Our smile at the idea of a peeress sitting in parliament, proceeds exactly from the same source. If the absurdity were in the intrinsic nature of the thing, most surely the position of our queen at her council-board would be more utterly absurd than that of a peeress in parliament. However, even the oddness and newness of the idea does not make it seem so ridiculous, but that the reviewer has been obliged to heighten the effect by making use of phraseology which tends to prepossess the mind. "Mixing with men in the stormy debates of a deliberative assembly," is not, we believe, a very faithful or exact description of what a peeress would do were she to sit in parliament, any more than it is of what our queen does in her council-chamber. Far from stormy debates being the order of the day in the House of Lords, we have always understood the peers to be at least remarkable for the order, propriety, and courtesy which prevail in their assembly. But we are not the advocate of the rights of peeresses, but of the rights of women; so shall pursue the subject only to add, that besides denying that there is anything inherently absurd in a peeress sitting and voting in parliament, we maintain that, even were that as absurd as our reviewer sets it down, it has little or no connexion with the point at issue, which is, whether women ought ever to be allowed a vote for a representative in parliament? It would have been more to the point had the dispute been, whether women should be allowed to sit as representatives in parliament?

We have no wish whatever to see women sitting as representatives; but, in saying this, we must not be misunderstood; for neither do we think it just to prevent them by law from doing do. There is very little prospect of women becoming very willing to accept the duties of legislators, and still less of bodies of electors becoming willing to accept them as representatives: so that there is no need of any law restraining them in this matter. In fact, in this as in every other respect, the natural restraints are enough: few women would consent to be chosen, and few electors would like to choose them; but still, if any individuals of the softer sex are able and willing to overleap the natural barriers, we see neither justice nor utility in opposing artificial ones to their progress.

In the general remarks to which the reviewer now proceeds, he expresses himself decidedly of opinion, that giving widows and spinsters the right of voting would not improve the social position of woman, but rather the reverse, by exciting a spirit of jealous opposition in man. We shall again quote a few words:—

"In all modern civilized communities, and especially in the most refined and cultivated portion of these communities, women are treated by men with peculiar deference, tenderness, and courtesy. Do they owe this treatment to their strength or their weakness? Undoubtedly to the latter."

Now, we cannot allow this at all. That woman does not owe any of the deference and tenderness with which she is treated to her physical strength, we can well believe. That she does owe them to her weakness, of any kind, we cannot see to be so apparent. We would rather hope that they are yielded her by man's increasing sense of the injustice of withholding them from her gentle and affectionate nature. Indeed, mildness, gentleness, and love, have a strength of their own, which has often, even in a feeble nature, been found capable of bidding defiance to all external agencies. And do not integrity and justice, even when disunited from any other force, or perhaps even the more for being exhibited by an otherwise feeble and helpless being, claim and receive an almost unlimited sympathy from the best and noblest of mankind? In these elements of strength the female character is by no means deficient. Nay, should it ever be proved that she is essentially inferior to man in intellectual power, perhaps the balance of their characters will be found in the superior strength of her affections and purity of her morals. It is not, then, to her weakness, but to her moral strength and influence, displayed and exercised in spite of her weakness, that woman owes all the advantages, worth retaining, which she at present enjoys. As for the deference paid to her weakness, the less she has of it the better. What is it but a premium held out by men—rendered foolish by the pride of having delicate and dependent creatures hanging upon them for support—to a most pernicious affectation of feebleness of body and silliness of mind? Let all that deference and courtesy which are due to the noble qualities of woman's nature be paid her, and not a shadow of respect to her weaknesses, and how much would woman be improved by the change! Nor do we fear that the courtesy now paid her would be thereby materially diminished; we believe, on the contrary, that it would gradually and surely increase.

If this question should come to be considered one of power, instead of one of justice, no one, we should think, could question the power of man to withhold the rights of woman: those rights must be upheld by man, or they will immediately fall to the ground. Since, then, woman must owe the maintenance of her rights to man's sense of the justice of her claims, not to any strength of her own—apart from the strength which a just claim imparts to the weakest claimant—we think there is little fear of the real tenderness of man towards woman being impaired; while we hope there would be a great diminution of that sickly affectation of helpless dependence, which the overweening pride of man now accepts as such a pleasant piece of flattery.

> ——"Then the loveliest in their fears,
> And by this silent adulation, soft,
> To their protection more engaging man."

But, although pleasing to his pride, the tenderness it excites must be a little mingled with contempt, especially if the helplessness—whether real or affected, or a mixture of both—be mental as well as physical. Assuredly, if a more self-relying and independent spirit were encouraged in woman, her companionship with man would be all the more ennobling for both. And would not even his pride be more nobly and generously gratified by seeing this apparently delicate and useless plaything elevated by his assistance, and sustained by his support in that dignified, useful, and comparatively independent position which, in our opinion, she was intended by nature to occupy? Yes! even the pride of man would, in this manner, be more nobly gratified than it will be by continuing to pay homage to the weaknesses of woman, till the whole sex are reduced to as complete a state of feebleness and silliness as the most empty and lordly of her masters could desire.

We hope, then, that our readers will agree with us, that the very circumstance of the inability of woman to support her own claims, and her necessary dependence upon man so far as the granting of those rights is concerned, will be a sufficient guarantee against the exercise of those rights exciting a spirit of jealous opposition in man, or at all diminishing the tenderness and courtesy which is now so willingly paid to woman.

We have now finished our examination of this article,—at least so far as the right of voting is concerned,— and trust that we have brought our readers to our own opinion, that the reasoning is to a very great degree weak and inconclusive. We should not have thought it worthy of being combated, had it not appeared in such a respectable and widely-circulated review. The circumstance of its appearance there led us to suspect that, contradictory and inconsequential as its line of reasoning was, yet that still it was as good as could be had on that side of the question; and our suspicions were confirmed by being unable to discover any other writer who has expressed the same opinions and whose arguments were more reasonable.

We are willing to believe that the weakness does not lie in these writers themselves, but in the opinions which they advocate. Should they be of a contrary opinion, they must exert themselves to discover more and better arguments; for they will find but few sensible people, who at all examine the matter, willing to submit to these.

CHAPTER IX.

INJUSTICE OF THE LAWS RELATING SPECIALLY TO WOMAN.

> "They [*his wife and children*]
> Neglected pine at home; themselves as more
> Exposed than others, with less scruple made
> His victims, robb'd of their defenceless all."
> *Cowper.*

> "Justice is lame, as well as blind amongst us;
> The laws corrupted to their ends that make them."
> *Venice Preserv'd.*

> "For what do heiress ever yet
> By being born to Lordships get?
> When the more Lady she's of Manors
> She's but exposed to more Trepanners."
> *Hudibras.*

We hope that we have now shown that our reasons for wishing to bestow equality of rights on both sexes are founded in nature, justice, and truth. But many whom we have so far brought along with us, may feel averse to the idea of change, and exclaim, that the present arrangements answer very well: that although women have had no share in making the laws, yet they have been made favourable for them. It may be asked what practical grievances they can complain of; putting out of the question the violation of their rights as reasonable and responsible beings, which is committed in enforcing, by the strong hand, obedience to laws, in the making of which they have had no share.

And this brings us naturally to the second great disadvantage attached to the lot of woman, namely, the evil and oppressive nature of the laws which have been enacted specially for her government. Of course by far the greater number of our laws apply to all, without distinction of sex; the penalty being the same whether the law be broken by a man or a woman. So far all is fair; and of this numerous class of laws we do not complain. Such laws as there may be either just or unjust; but, at all events, they make no partial distinctions between the sexes. If they be oppressive, it is not with regard to one sex at the expense of the other;

they bear equally hard upon both. These, then, being out of our range, we shall take no farther notice of them, but confine ourselves to the consideration of those comparatively few laws which have been enacted for the special guidance of women, and of which we conceive that there is just ground for great complaint.

When the representatives of man alone legislate between man and woman, we know enough of the deceitfulness of the human heart, and of the usual nature of class legislation, even did the laws which have been made not bear witness, to have some fear that these laws would not be of the most impartial order. It is perfectly natural, even were all the men concerned in the legislation as just as Aristides, which was not very likely to be the case, that, at least, when the decision was in any degree doubtful, they should give it in favour of their own sex. Legislators, as well as poets, have talked very prettily about the right of woman to support and protection from man; but their gallant and chivalrous sentiments have usually ended in talk, or, at least, in kind affectionate behaviour to the female members of their respective families. They have taken little care that woman's rights should have any firmer basis of support than the arbitrary will of that man—husband, father, or whatever other relative—who happens to be her guardian for the time.

The inability of a married woman to hold property—except it be bound to her before marriage by expensive deeds—is a law which is most evidently the result of class legislation, and which occasions much misery. The fortune, whether large or small, of an heiress is, at present, not so much her own property as a sort of perquisite attached to her person; whoever obtains her as a wife, by whatever means, obtains from that moment complete possession of all her property: it is no longer her own,—she is now reduced to entire dependence on her husband. So completely is it alienated from her, that even in case of her husband's death it does not revert to her,—by far the greatest proportion of it going to her husband's heirs, although these heirs should not be her children, and most probably entire strangers to her. If she has children, it is true that these will, in most cases, be her husband's heirs; but no one likes to be obliged to give up his property, even in favour of his own child. Now, if it be hard to give up one's property, even to those who are dearest to us, how must the hardship be increased to a woman who has no children. Upon her husband's death, she must see most part of their mutual property taken possession of by comparative strangers,—very distant relatives of her husband coming before her as heirs, although, previously to her marriage, the property was exclusively her own.

It is to this essentially-unjust law that we owe all those attempts—too often successful—of unprincipled adventurers, to gain possession of those unfortunate young women who are nominally left heiresses—but really are a sort of burden attached—to large possessions. How often does a man enter into what ought to be the most sacred of all connexions, simply to possess himself of the fortune of an heiress, without the slightest feeling of affection for herself! And, when this is the case, he will be pretty sure to let her feel how galling the dependence is to which she is reduced. She, on the contrary, young, artless, unsuspicious, had no motive save affection for forming this connexion,—the idea of mercenary motives in her partner never glanced across her mind. What tortured feelings must she endure, then, on the discovery, so sure to be made, that her fortune was her sole charm in her lover's eyes, and that now he regards her as an absolute encumbrance! If, seeing that her fate is now fixed, she tries to accommodate herself to it, her patience and submission seem only to invite farther indifference and indignity. He now no longer pretends to conceal that another engages those affections which were never hers. If, at last, when insult and ill treatment are no longer endurable, she wishes to leave his abode, a scanty pittance out of what ought to be her own and her children's fortune is all that the law allots for her support.

But this is not all,—her children, as well as her fortune, are the property of her husband. They are torn from her maternal arms, and remain at *his* absolute disposal, who "hates and wrongs" their mother, "the woman he has sworn to love and cherish." He may, if he chooses, confide the care of their nurture to the tender mercies of the rival of their mother, though she be the most licentious of her sex. In company with her he may waste the substance of the family in riotous living; and, after having ruined the morals of his children, may complete their destruction by casting them adrift upon the world.

It is true that the *Custody of Infants' Bill* has recently undergone some revision, by which matters are a little improved; but by no means to the extent which would constitute impartial justice between the sexes. What we have stated is still the law; it is only improved in so far that, whereas formerly it was quite absolute, it now admits of appeal. The chancellor has now a discretionary power of giving the wife the charge of her children if he sees fit; but, as long as the laws continue in force which prevent married women from holding property, this power of appeal will be of very little use: for the husband has possession, in the first instance; and it is only after a tedious and expensive process, which few women in this situation have a sufficient command of funds to carry on, that her children can be restored to her, if ever they are restored at all.

The hardships which fall upon a woman in such a case, from her inability to hold property, are no doubt great, both as respects herself and her children; but they are by no means the worst consequences which may be, and often are, the result of these unjust laws. As no industry of her own produced the property of an heiress, so it is not nearly such a hardship for her to lose it, as it is for the hard-working, industrious woman to lose the fruit of her own labour: yet, such is the law. The produce of a married woman's labour does not belong to herself: it is the property of her husband. He may take it, without any leave from her, and waste it in dissipation and excess. There is many a woman cursed with a husband who, instead of being the protector, is the robber and oppressor of his family. Idle, drunken, dissolute, he throws on his wife the whole burden of providing both for themselves and their children. Nay, the law considering her earnings as his property, and thereby allowing him to rob her with impunity, he is not ashamed to take every opportunity of appropriating to himself and his own disgraceful pleasures what his wife has exerted herself to obtain for the support of their family.

Let a woman, by the hard-won earnings of her honest industry, place her family in comparative comfort in spite of the heavy drawback of such a *helpmate* as we have described; let her, in spite of all her difficulties, save a little money to be applied to some cherished object—perhaps the education of her children; let her do all this, and more if she can,—but let her not expect long to enjoy the fruits of her virtuous exertions. By the laws of her country, those household goods which enable her to see her children happy and comfortable around her, and the frugal savings she has destined for their education, do not belong to her. They are the property of her husband; whenever he pleases he can take possession of her all, though gained by the work of her own hands. This is no imaginary case. Many women have been robbed in this manner, not once, but repeatedly; and in these trying circumstances have been known to exert such unwearied patience, fortitude, and industry, as might well put to the blush the detractors of the sex. To continue steadfastly going forward in the path of duty, in spite of the heart-crushing effects of such oppression, requires, in our opinion, greater courage and a nobler spirit than to face an army.

In that article in *The Edinburgh Review* to which we have had occasion so often to advert, the writer is candid enough to allow that there are many real causes of complaint in the state of the law with regard to women. He especially mentions the laws about property between husband and wife; but seems to think that the grounds of dissatisfaction are about equal on both sides. We shall let him speak for himself.

"With respect to property, there is a lamentable want of due protection against the effects of extravagance and vice; and the law is impartial only in its balance of injustice, and in allowing to the culpable of either sex the most unbridled impunity in wrong-doing. The extravagant wife may contract debts for which her husband may be sent to prison. The vicious husband of an heiress, whose friends or legal advisers may have been careless or inefficient, and failed in securing her just rights by settlement previous to marriage, may plunge her into utter ruin, by squandering, in spite of her most earnest remonstrances, her patrimony upon his own pleasures."

Of course that law must be on a bad principle which allows the "just rights" of any class to depend upon the carelessness or the efficiency of friends and advisers. Why is any settlement required to secure the rights of an heiress after marriage? A general law, which would apply to each individual of this class, would surely be much better, and secure their just rights more effectually, than trusting to each party securing her own interests by a treaty especially for herself.

At the first glance, and read without reflection, the passage I have quoted seems to show that, in the disposition of property, the law, if not just, is at least impartial to the sexes; but a little consideration will convince us that this is hardly the truth. The incapacity of a married woman to hold property is the root from whence all the evils complained of spring. The responsibility of her husband for her debts is a necessary consequence of the injustice which deprives her of her fortune and gives it to him. As a woman on her marriage loses all right to property, all right even to the earnings of her own hands, of course she cannot be held responsible even for her own debts; and who ought to be responsible but the person who profits by the wrong done her in the first instance? The wrong done woman is evidently the greatest. That done man is slight— as there are few men who cannot restrain an extravagant woman; and were it greater, it would be well merited by the injustice which has been the origin of it. Were a husband not entitled to more than a half of his wife's property, then an heiress could not be ruined by a spendthrift husband; and she, of course, would be responsible for her own debts. And were a wife entitled to some certain share of her husband's property, (as really and personally as a husband now is entitled to the whole of his wife's,) then, again, she would be held responsible for her own debts, and her husband never could be imprisoned for her.

We think it absurd, when talking of a great wrong done, to speak as if that wrong, and a little inconvenience suffered in consequence by the wrong-doer, balanced each other—as if the person who suffered the wrong had nothing to complain of, because the wrong-doer did not gain unmingled good by his evil deeds. It is as if the robber should complain of the trouble of carrying off and disposing of his stolen goods, and assert that that trouble balanced accounts between him and the person robbed.

The instances we have mentioned in illustration may be thought extreme and isolated cases; but it was necessary to choose such as would bring out the case clearly and distinctly; and, extreme and isolated as they appear, they are such as the records of our courts of justice show to be of frequent occurrence. Such instances of oppression and injustice as these, while at first sight they seem to stand apart from the current of society, like the great men, whether good or bad, of any age, are, like these great men, but a more prominent representation of the spirit of that society which has produced them. This consideration shows us, in the most striking point of view, the all-spreading evil—the leprosy—so to speak, which these wicked and unjust laws have generated. This will also be seen very clearly, if we consider how much oppression women in general will endure before appealing to law: so that we may be sure that there is abundance of tyranny exercised over women which is never made public.

There is no class of unjust laws which has exercised a more degrading influence on the human mind than the laws with regard to property on the mind of woman. They have given birth to that spirit, so general, which makes a wife consider herself merely as the steward of her husband,—or even less than steward, for she gets no wages. Hence the spirit of trickery and cheating is introduced, and appropriating to themselves, or spending in a different manner from that which they represent to their husbands, the funds with which he provides them. The reader will find this dissimulation, and giving in of false accounts, spoken of by Mrs Hall, in a tale in "Chambers's Edinburgh Journal," called the "Private Purse," as a thing of very common, not to say general practice. We hope there is more honesty among wives than Mrs Hall gives them credit for; but certainly we should be more grieved than surprised to meet with something to convince us that she is correct in her representation. Although cases of dishonesty and deceit may be more rare—and from our own observation we should certainly conclude that they were—than Mrs Hall seems to think; yet we believe that the spirit which leads to those gross vices—that is, a spirit of servility and dependence, a feeling by wives that none of their husband's property belongs strictly to themselves—is as general as she represents it, and as she seems to think it ought to be.

Now this feeling, so abject and degrading in itself, and so capable of leading to meanness, dissimulation, and all manner of dishonesty, is the produce of unjust laws in the regulation of property; and it is this wide-spread and hardly discernible evil which is by far their most pernicious result.

For our part, we would have every woman regard her husband's property as *bonâ fide* her own. We would have her as soon think of cheating herself as her husband, with any pretences or false accounts whatever; and that, not because she considered herself as his steward and was faithful to him, but because she considered herself an equal partner, and never doubted the propriety of spending the money allotted to her department in the manner she judged most proper. Of course no woman ought to spend her money in any way which she would be ashamed to acknowledge to her husband or to any one: and when she has money given to her for a specific purpose, she ought, certainly, to apply it to that purpose; but in the general management of the house expenses, and whatever else she takes charge of, the mistress of a family ought always to feel and act with the utmost freedom and independence. If any man wishes in his wife a mere servant, who is to give a strict account of every farthing he doles out to her, he will act but wisely in so far removing temptation from her, as to give her the wages when he invests her with the character of a servant; for every one feels a sort of necessity for some little sum upon which he can exercise his own discretion. This necessity assists greatly to tempt so many women (not considering the money with which they are entrusted by their husbands as their own) to the pitiful deceit of setting apart a portion of this allowance for their own private use, and giving a false account of this portion. Thus an entrance is given to all sorts of lying and dissimulation; and the tortuous path of falsehood once entered, it is impossible to tell in what gulf of sin and misery it may not end.

We must here make ourselves distinctly understood. We would have every woman regard the whole sum she has at her disposal as we fancy these dishonest women do the sum which they abstract, and take the same care to lay it out to advantage as if it were strictly her own. We can, however, see no harm whatever in a woman having a private purse, as it is called; in other words, being perfectly independent of her husband for her own personal expenses. Nor do we see any harm in a wife—supposing she has no private property of her own—dividing the sum entrusted to her by her husband, and holding part of it in trust, as it were, for her family, and setting another apart for her own dress and personal expenses. We consider that the dishonest women do nothing wrong, so far as the setting aside of a certain sum for their own particular use is concerned; no! the wrong is in the falsehood, and perhaps also in the setting apart, for this purpose, a larger sum than is justifiable, on considering the whole income, and the many other uses to which it has to be applied; which is indeed very likely to be the source whence the falsehood springs. Conscious of selfishness, they are ashamed to confess it. Now we would have women so to lay out their money that they would rather feel pleasure than shame in allowing their husbands to look over all, even their most private accounts, though they were quite independent of him. We would have them to act with rectitude as well as independence.

What we mean, then, by the servile and abject spirit which the laws about property have produced in woman, will, we hope, be clearly understood. And we consider this wide-spread and abasing feeling as a much greater evil, and much more fatal to virtue and even to happiness, than those prominent instances of injustice which we have used to show more strikingly the flagrant iniquity of those laws of which we complain.

It is, perhaps, more difficult to alter laws which affect property than almost any other; but though difficult, it is not impossible; and these laws call aloud for revision. Instead of "with all my worldly goods I thee endow," a bridegroom, to speak in accordance with the laws, ought to say "what is yours, is mine; and what is mine, is *my own*." We have thrown out a hint that the joint property of a wedded pair—whether it belonged originally to the husband or to the wife, or whether it is the produce of the husband's labour or the wife's—ought to belong, not as it now practically does to one party alone, but really and truly, in some certain and fair proportion, to both parties; and, in cases of separation—due regard being paid to the maintenance of the children—to be divided accordingly. But this is merely to be considered as a very rough hint: we do not mean it at all as a proposal of any measure, but simply to give some little indication of what we would consider just. Any change affecting so many different interests, must necessarily require to be maturely considered, and in many different points of view.

If the laws which regulate property be thus partial and unjust, the regulations for trials, either civil or criminal, in which women are concerned, are at least equally so. Trial by a jury of the peers of the parties interested, is the great boast of British jurisprudence. We would ask, was there ever a woman tried by a jury of her peers? Small, indeed, is the benefit which she derives from that noble institution. What renders her case in this instance the harder, is the consideration that most of the causes in which women are interested, which come before juries, are causes which may be supposed, in a peculiar degree, to excite the party spirit—so to speak— of sex. In cases of the assault or murder of husbands by their wives—alas! that such things are—is to be expected that a jury of men will pay the same attention to the palliations of the dreadful catastrophe—such as the misery produced by long-endured, but at last unendurable insult and cruelty—as if the case were reversed. We must say, that to us it seems impossible that the palliations can come so home to their hearts in this case as they would were it reversed. And there are many like cases. Indeed, it is seldom that a jury have to decide between two women; almost always it is between a man and a woman, when a woman is at all implicated in the case.

Such are specimens of the fairness of those laws which the so-much-boasted influence of woman has been able to obtain from the gallantry—for it is to the gallantry rather than the justice of man that the influence of woman appeals—of her generous lord. Surely little comment upon these laws is necessary. It is merely required that attention be called to them, and some indication given of the countless oppressions—beyond the reach of law to remedy—which have been occasioned by the universal diffusion in society of the spirit which pervades them; and, worse than all, to point out the spirit of cunning, dishonesty, and dissimulation—the meanness and servility of mind which it is their direct tendency to create and foster in woman. When all these things are taken into account, surely it will be allowed that the truth has not been overstepped by the assertion, that woman is not represented: these laws would certainly have been modified had she been so: or, by the other assertion, that the want of representation has been an occasion of wronging her, these laws are certainly unjust.

CHAPTER X.

EDUCATION.

"Our most important are our earliest years;
The mind impressible and soft, with ease
Imbibes and copies what she hears and sees;
And through life's labyrinth holds fast the clew
Which education gives her, false or true."
Cowper.

"Woman, whom custom has forbid to fly
The scholar's pitch (the scholar best knows why.)"
Cowper.

We now come to the last great disadvantage under which the women of this country manifestly labour—namely, the want of the means, or, at least, the great difficulty of obtaining the means of a good substantial education; occasioned, in a great measure, by public neglect and indifference.

The incalculable greatness of the evil influence which ignorance in its women must bring to bear on any community, and the evident tendency of a race of truly enlightened women to produce, in their turn, a more enlightened race of men, are certainly very good public reasons for the discontinuance of this system towards women. But far from being the only reasons—as is often assumed—neither of these is the best or truest argument for doing away with a system so partial and injurious. The intrinsic value of a human soul, and its infinite capability of improvement, are the true reasons for the culture of any human being, woman no less than man. The grand plea for woman sharing with man all the advantages of education is, that every rational being is worthy of cultivation, for his or her own individual sake. The first object in the education of every mind ought to be its own development. Doubtless, the improvement of the influence exerted upon others will be a necessary consequence; but it ought never to be spoken of as the first inducement to it. It is too much the custom, even of the most liberal in these matters, to urge the education and enlightenment of women, rather as a means of improving *man*, than as, in itself, an end of intrinsic excellence, which certainly seems to us the first and greatest consideration.

If woman be naturally more feeble of intellect than man, surely she has, on that very account, the greater need of all the advantages which education can bestow. What appearance is there, then, of great care having been taken to improve the soft and feeble character of her mind? Has a strengthening and envigorating system of education been provided for her? The defects of her mental powers having been so obvious, doubtless there are plenty of schools and colleges endowed for her benefit, that as far as possible these deficiencies might be remedied? No, indeed! this is very far from being the case. Should this being, said to be so feeble of intellect, feel any desire after knowledge, any impulse to advance farther than the mere alphabet of learning, difficulties multiply around her at every step. As might be expected, in the usual course of class legislation, almost all the public money given in aid of education is employed in removing obstacles from the path of that sex which possesses the power of granting the money; and the individual members of which, if they be so much stronger of intellect as they pretend to be, are more able to remove obstacles for themselves, or to advance in spite of them.

In almost every town of a few thousand inhabitants, there are endowed schools for the benefit of the sons of citizens; but in almost every case the daughters are entirely neglected. That is, neglected in a public sense. We do not mean to say, they are neglected by their individual parents: such instruction as these can procure for them, we dare say they do; but there is no combination—no laying of heads together—no public care, in short, is taken to provide means for the education of girls, as is done for that of boys. This inattention and indifference we consider to be an evil of which the sex may justly complain. It is a grievance which, besides being unfair in itself, leads to evils and prejudices which run through the whole even of that system of more private instruction which girls do receive.

Besides the want of any public attention to the providing of first-rate elementary schools for girls, there is a great want of such institutions as colleges for young women of the higher ranks who have plenty of leisure; and even of the lower ranks who have a strong desire to pursue their studies diligently and with little liability to interruption. The want of any institutions such as these, where women might pursue in quiet retirement the cultivation of their minds to any extent they might wish, besides its immediate ill effects in throwing unprepared into the bustle and battle of society the individual women who would have delighted to profit by it, has inflicted an indefinite portion of evil on the education of all; by introducing the notion, that any depth of knowledge is beyond the grasp of a woman's mind. Her instruction has been modified accordingly; so that, when she does make progress, it is in spite of a thousand more obstacles than those which stand in the path of man.*

It is this which makes it so difficult to decide positively that the sexes really are unequal in their mental powers. We should say, that the evident advantages over woman, both in means of culture and opportunity of developing his powers, which the physical superiority of man has given him, makes it very difficult, if possible, to *prove* the mental inferiority of woman. It may have taken as much mental power for woman to make the progress she has done, in spite of those obstacles which her inferiority in physical strength has thrown in her path, as it has done to advance man to his present position, with the numerous advantages which his superior strength has given him.

Even in the case of genius, (which it has been urged† ought to show itself with the same freedom and force in woman as in man, were there not some radical inferiority in the texture of her mind,) it may reasonably be asked—would not this greatest of gifts have done more for woman than it ever has done for man, had it raised one of a sex so depressed and subdued to a level with the genius which has been shown forth among men? What man of genius is there who has not been greatly influenced, not to say almost formed, by the age in which he lived, the nation and rank in which he was born, and the education he received? Men of genius may be the leaders of their age; but as certainly they never get beyond it in every respect. Genius in woman will certainly be subject to an equal degree of influence from surrounding outward causes as in man; and is not the constant trammeling of the mind of woman as important and as depreciatory an influence as is necessary to account for all the difference we perceive in the manifestation of genius in man and woman?

* There is one educational opportunity which might very easily be afforded to ladies, and which we have often regretted their very unnecessary exclusion from, we mean the liberty of attending the meetings of those literary and philosophical societies which now exist in most considerable towns. What pleasure, and even instruction, might they not derive from accompanying their friends to such meetings. If either their natural diffidence or defective education should hinder them from joining in the discussions or speculations carried on at such meetings, yet, we are quite sure that many of the female relatives of literary men would relish hearing them as much as their husbands or brothers possibly could enjoy taking part in them. And what harm could their presence occasion? We can see no greater impropriety in the different sexes seeking intellectual instruction or entertainment in company with each other, than in their enjoying each other's society in any other pursuit.

† See *Edinburgh Review* on the Rights and Condition of Woman.

There have been women in every department of life—in which women were at all suffered to appear—who have shown genius second only to the highest genius in man. And it might fairly be questioned whether, but for those depressing influences which it is too evident have always, in many ways, borne down the intellectual powers of woman, she would not have stood on a level with the very highest. If the noblest and stoutest hearted among men have been powerless to extricate themselves entirely from the errors and prejudices of the age, the country, the very city and family in which they dwelt,—was a greater power of self-emancipation to be looked for in the case of individuals of a sex whose physical weakness had given it over for ages to the absolute dominion of man? The woman of genius has hitherto in no respect more truly represented her sex than in its subjugation. She has shown us glimpses of a better order of things; but glimpses only. But this is exactly what one might have predicted from a knowledge of the circumstances; it is perfectly natural, and ought not therefore to be at all regretted or wondered at. Even men of genius are seldom or never citizens of the world: they are Englishmen, Italians, Germans, as the case may be; and it is no more matter of surprise that women of genius have shared the thraldom of their sex, than that even men of genius do not get quit of national peculiarities.

But besides this, woman is not altogether and only *woman*, she is also *man*; a lesser man (as one of our present poets calls her) if you will, but still man. She partakes the nature of the greatest men, as much as the ordinary race of men partake that nature. She assists the development of genius perhaps even more than man, and certainly appreciates it as truly and keenly. Even should a stronger physical framework than she possesses be required for the manifestation of the highest genius, she is not thereby cut off from that genius by an impassable gulf, any more than that numerous class of men, inferior in little save the power of articulating the thoughts which brood in their inmost souls,—and these alone can appreciate properly the creations of genius,—who find in its very highest and noblest flights, only a true and clear interpretation of ideas which are more darkly flitting through their own minds, but which they have not sufficient energy to grasp and delineate to others.

Even in man, the manifestation of the highest genius is very rare; and woman, to say the least, falls short only of that highest manifestation; and is, therefore, not much worse off, in this respect, than all men who fall short of that highest genius. Shakspere, Homer, Milton—all great men—belong as truly to her as to the rest of mankind. The true, beautiful, and noble thoughts which genius is privileged to give utterance to, finds as faithful an echo in the soul of woman as in that of man. What woman, in studying the outward manifestations of genius, does not lose all consciousness of sex, and take home, to the inmost depths of her heart, those ideas which are addressed indeed to man, but which she feels apply to her, whatever she is; and which are really but articulate expressions of what she feels to be part and parcel of her own nature? Who can admire and sympathize with genius more than woman? And in what other respect, save in deepest sympathy and admiration, do ordinary men show that they are akin to the great of their race. Had women read, and taken to heart as their guides in life, only those writings which have been addressed to themselves, what a miserable figure would they now make in society,—how far short would their progress be of what it now is! But it has not been so. Whatever deep, holy, and beautiful truths have been written by and addressed to man, have also become known to many among women; and in learning them, woman has felt that she has not been learning something utterly foreign to herself; she has felt herself for the time a man, and really is one, as far as finding a response in her own bosom to all the noblest aspirations of man can constitute her one. And what else constitutes ordinary men the kinsmen of the man of genius?

The great deficiencies, in point of education, which woman has hitherto had to contend with, will, we think, be readily allowed; although the writer in *The Edinburgh Review*, whose article we have already mentioned, doubts this deficiency very much, and seems inclined to think that girls are, if anything, better educated than boys. He excuses himself from speaking of education as it is at present carried on,—the great changes which have been going on of late years making it not very easy to pronounce any opinion upon it; he, therefore, takes the first thirty years of the present century, and remarks:

"We firmly believe that, in a vast majority of cases, the girl of seventeen was better informed upon such subjects as well-educated persons ought to be conversant with—possessed of a more cultivated understanding, and more capable of conversing intelligently with persons much older than herself—than the boy of the same age. If this be so—and though no proof can be offered in support of such assertion, we confidently make it in the belief that there are few of our readers who will not concur with us—it cannot be urged with any plausibility, that to education rather than to nature man owes that mental superiority over woman, the existence of which cannot be denied.

"It may be argued, on the other side, that this is true on the assumption that education ceases at the early age of seventeen; but this is scarcely true with regard to either sex,—for at this period, or a little later, frequently begins the most valuable part of a young man's education, when comparatively free from the trammels of strict superintendence and the compulsory imposition of distasteful tasks, but animated with a zeal for the acquisition of knowledge which he believes would be beneficial to him, he begins to educate himself. In this there is much truth; and in this sense, far from being limited to the period of youth, education never ceases; for every acquisition of knowledge by an individual for himself, as long as his faculties are capable of acquiring, may be included under that term. But to use education in this sense, and to reason upon it as if it were identical with the instruction which young persons derive from their elders, is to deceive ourselves by similarity of term. * * * *
No: if the superiority gained by men is referable chiefly to self-education, we must go farther, and admit that it is ultimately referable to that natural strength of intellect, without which self-education would not have been effectual."

There is such an intermingling of truth and error in all this, that one hardly knows where to take it. To begin, however, at the beginning, we would remark that it is very possible that at seventeen a girl may be as much better informed than a boy as is here represented, and yet that the comparatively uninformed boy may be better intellectually educated. For what is a good intellectual education? it is not, certainly, the learning a certain number of facts, although that also may be necessary. No: education is not so much the knowledge which the mind acquires, as the direction which is given to that mind; and whatever progress the girl of seventeen may have made in knowledge, if she has been taught to look forward to that period as the end or *finishing*, as it is called, of her education, she is much worse educated than the boy, though he may now be far behind her in general information, who has been taught to consider his present studies as the mere foundation of that learning which his early manhood is to be devoted to the attainment of.

This line of argument either excludes—very unjustifiably—from all consideration, that large class of young men who receive direct instruction from their superiors in universities long after the age of seventeen; or it asserts, that a college education and self-instruction are identical. We think the usual opinion is, that these are the opposites of each other; and confess that in this we are inclined to follow the multitude. Certainly, we think the instruction which a youth receives at the university, though of course less compulsory than that which he received when a boy at school, is still of the same nature,—still to be classed with that instruction which young people receive from their elders. And where is the counterpart to this most valuable part of the education of young men to be found in the education of young women of the same class of society to which these young men usually belong? No counterpart to this is found in the education of any class of young women. When a young man leaves school, he is said to be prepared for college. When a girl leaves school, he education is said to be *finished*; and in that phrase one of the evil influences which pervade the education of girls may be seen.

Soon after the young woman leaves school, she is in most cases introduced to society, and immediately thrown into a position the most unfavourable for study. Gaieties and amusements of all kinds press themselves upon her. Even should she herself despise a life devoted to these, she will, in general, meet with little sympathy from her friends, should she wish to relinquish them for more solid and satisfying pursuits. Very many parents would think their daughter's education had been mismanaged, and reprimand her severely for having let slip the opportunities she had enjoyed at school, should she, feeling that her mind is a rich soil, which only requires cultivation to repay the labour ten-fold, presume to hint, after that age, that she still feels oppressed by ignorance, and wishes her mind again set to work. Very far, indeed, from receiving those aids and encouragements, not to mention that direct instruction which a university education affords to young men, a girl of seventeen is taught to believe that, if her education is not now finished, she is very backward indeed, and that she has abused the opportunities of instruction which her parents afforded her.

How is all this reversed with young men? They leave school, indeed, about the same time; but far from regarding their education as finished, they have been all this time taught that they are laying the foundation for that most valuable part of their education which is now to commence. They are now introduced, not into the bustle and distractions of the world, but into the calm and quiet of a venerable university, where every inducement is offered them to continue their studies with diligence, and every means is provided to ensure that this pursuit will be successful. Their faculties have arrived at a degree of maturity; their teachers are the most learned men, and well experienced in the art of communicating knowledge; books on all subjects are at their command. Learning is the recognised business of this part of their lives. They have leisure, in quiet retirement, to take advantage of all this abundance of the means of culture.

Is it, then, anything like a fair inference, that girls receive, on the whole, a better education than boys, because, at a certain age, they have acquired more general information than boys? Is it not a still more unfair statement, that it is the education which young men *give themselves* after leaving school which constitutes the chief difference in the education of the sexes; and, of course, that if young women do not bestow on themselves the same culture, the blame rests wholly on the inferior nature of their minds, which will not undertake such labour? The truer statement of the case would be—boys are taught to consider their school exercises as the foundation on which a superstructure is to be reared, and there are plenty of means to assist them in carrying on the building. Girls are in a manner disgraced if they do not rear the whole flimsy structure in the same time which is given the others merely to lay the foundation; and even if they had a solid foundation laid at school, have only very scanty material and irregular opportunities to carry on the work afterwards. We think, then— and we hope that few, on considering the matter, will refuse to go along with us— that it is exceedingly unfair to talk as if the sexes had equal opportunities for developing their intellectual nature, but that one sex was incapable of profiting by these means of culture.

Even were the admission made—which, however, we are far from allowing—that if woman had the same intellectual strength as man, she would, ere this, have burst the barriers of prejudice, and created for herself those "appliances and means" of intellectual culture which have hitherto been confined almost exclusively to the use of man;—even this admission would be no reason why any one should argue as if she did possess the means, and was indolent and dilatory in the use of them. Neither would it be any reason why she should not owe to the justice or generosity of man, those aids to the cultivation and development of her nature which she has not had vigour enough to achieve for herself.

That she does make many attempts to advance in spite of all these obstacles, is evident from the very respectable figure she has made in modern literature. De Stael, Hemans, Edgeworth, Baillie, Morgan, Martineau, More, Somerville, are names taken almost at random from a host of female writers who have certainly been much above mediocrity, even of manly talent. Thus we see that many women struggle on in the work of self-culture, in spite of every obstacle; and a few even contrive to show some outward manifestation of their success; but it is very little to be wondered at if even these honourable few should partake in some measure of the long-continued mental thraldom of their sex. Kept down and depressed on all sides by the usages of society, it is little wonder if the works even of women of genius show, in some degree, the characteristics of the author's sex, and seldom or never exhibit that frank and fearless originality which characterizes genius in man.

Although these remarks apply particularly only to that limited number who attend college, and receive as thorough an education as these institutions can afford them,—still it will be found, that this high cultivation of a part of the one sex, in which no part of the other sex is allowed to partake, gives men, as a whole, a weight and authority, which, we must be excused for saying, we think they are not at all scrupulous, but, on the contrary, most ungenerous and unjust, in using to lower the intellect of woman in public estimation. A thousand little slighting remarks, which a candid person would at once see applied with equal force to a part of both sexes, but not at all to the whole of either, are made and applied without hesitation, as a matter of course, to *all* women. How often do we see such depreciatory remarks introduced casually, and perhaps thoughtlessly—for it has come to be almost a matter of custom—in the works of men who have themselves, in spite of their sex, been a thousand fold surpassed by individuals of that softer sex which they consign with such a lordly air to wholesale contempt. We could easily produce many examples of this, even from writers of the present day; but refrain, because such a multitude of quotations would be required to prove that it is so common as we believe it to be, and also, because we think we may very safely appeal for the support of our position to the memory of any reader of general literature. Those slighting remarks upon woman have some effect, by mere iteration, even upon those who would see and acknowledge their extreme unfairness, if called on to think about the matter; but their authority is almost unbounded with that large class of men—and we might add of women also—who hold the contemptuous opinion of the sex which are still but too common.

Of course, the greatest contrast in the education of the sexes is in those classes where the sons receive a university education; but, even in the middle and lower classes, the instruction which the girls receive is, we believe, on the whole, inferior both in quantity and quality; while there is an utter impossibility of the instruction of individuals being extended on the exhibition of any unusual talent,—an advantage which individual boys of the lower class frequently receive, through the devoted affection of their friends, on their displaying any extraordinary application to learning. There is indeed, we believe, provision made in most universities for the gratuitous admission to the academic course of at least a few young men of this description.

But even those young men who enter into business at seventeen, have numerous educational opportunities at their command after that period, from which young women are almost if not entirely shut out. Evening classes and lectures for young men in business are now very numerously attended, and replace, in some degree, the want of a college education.

In general, when a girl returns from school, the only way in which she can continue her education is by private study—we might almost say stolen study—in the midst of continual distractions and interruptions. Those only who are very earnest will continue their studies long. Many very soon leave them off, and many more never think of them at all, but sink contented, at seventeen, into that elegant nothing—a finished young lady. If woman's mind is so feeble, why is she left to struggle with all those difficulties which are so sedulously removed from the path of man? Why are there not great public institutions for young women to attend, that they may have every assistance in carrying on the work of self-culture, when they arrive at the proper age for it, instead of being forced, as they now are, to struggle on alone and unaided; or if they have not energy enough for that, having recourse to novels, embroidery, working in worsted, or some such kill-time occupation?

If, instead of looking at the amount of actual instruction provided for the young, we look to the spirit which pervades that instruction, we shall find the education of young women as defective in this as it is deficient in the former. A proper education may be stated shortly to be that training which assists the mind to look into itself, which enables it to see its own powers and to use them effectively. Now, the education of girls, whatever facts it may teach them, does not, we think, tend to expand and develop their minds, but to cramp and confine them. Far from being encouraged to use their own faculties, any symptom of independent thought is quickly repressed. The consequence, as might be expected, is, that the majority of girls are subdued into mere automatons,—their very excellencies are not made their own, by being powerfully grasped by their own minds; they are rather the physical effect of example and habit, than the result of the exercise of their own moral and intellectual nature. Hence, many women pass a considerable portion of their lives with great apparent propriety, paying even more than due submission to the guardian—be he husband, brother, or father—who happens to have charge of the grown baby. Yet if any strong passion, such as love, jealousy, or hatred, takes possession of her mind, she will allow it to burst forth with such fury, as manifestly to show that her former good conduct was quite mechanical, and proceeded from no firm principle rooted in her mind. Nay, we have observed in every such case, that the more submissive and subservient a woman has been before such an outburst of passion, the more perfectly does she show a want of all self-control when it is required. The effect of the common system of female education is to produce a mechanical performance of duty, converting women into mere machines; so that all the good they do is towards others, their own minds all the while lying barren and unfruitful. For our part, we would rather see a few errors in routine, if accompanied with the true self-improving spirit, than the most faultless exterior of mechanical performance of duty, convinced that, in any emergency out of the usual routine, the first would stand fast and the last would utterly fail.

We confess we feel strongly the evil of the tendency of female education to produce a mere automaton—a subdued, passive tool, which the elements of society fashion outwardly, but which has no inward power to seize upon those elements and convert them into means of growth, both moral and intellectual. What, to give an instance, can be more improving for a woman's whole nature than the faithful and life-like discharge of the duties of a wife and mother? Yet, how often do we see those duties performed tolerably well, to all outward appearance, while the soul is in the deepest slumber. When these duties are performed in this matter-of-course sort of way—with the least possible exertion of the powers of the mind, rather in a negative sense doing no evil than positively doing good—they produce not half the good of which they are capable on the mother's own mind, and leave it to almost complete stagnation when her children no longer require her attention. This cold, hard, mechanical, loveless, spiritless performance of duty, is, in a very great measure, the manner in which even a good mother now goes about her work, lifeless and soulless in comparison of what we would see were her whole moral and intellectual nature wakened up, and engaged with enlightened earnestness in that work, which would, at the same time, be giving life and health, and development, to her own soul. And who could estimate the effects of such an improvement upon education in general?—But all our laws and public institutions, as well as the education of woman, and the tone of conversation in regard to her, tend to subdue and trammel her mind, to deprive it of all self-reliance, to keep even its individual being out of sight, and reduce it to a mere appendage of man. Well may we assert with a recent writer, that woman is "taught to believe, that for one half of the human race, the highest end of civilisation is to cling upon the other, like a weed upon a wall."

Born to the endurance of constant control from the irresponsible power exercised over her by man, she is early trained to implicit submission. But were the limits of this arbitrary power a little better defined, and woman encouraged to be somewhat more independent and self-relying, then her actions, springing from the exercise of her own faculties, would bring into use a thousand powers of mind which her sleepy reliance on the judgment of others too often allows to lie dormant.

Is it not even cruel, in the present state of society, to *educate* woman for this state of dependence? Will not the very physical weakness of her sex too much incline her to rely implicitly on a stronger than herself? And when we consider how far that stronger is from perfect virtue, would it not be well that the education of woman should tend to fortify her mind, teach her not to rely implicitly on so erring a guide, and impress her with her own individual responsibility. The wisdom of this course is seen more clearly in the consideration, that even this erring guide is denied to woman. How often do we see her thrown entirely on her own resources by the misfortunes or wickedness of her natural protectors, or by being deprived of them altogether. Nor would a woman make a worse wife—to any but a vitiated taste—or mother, by being provided with some inward springs of peace and satisfaction—as well as some motives to activity, both physical and mental—should the great sources of happy employment to woman be denied her. Her present education hinders her from performing her most common and natural duties efficiently; and, at the same time, deprives her of very many means of pleasure and activity in the lonely condition to which she is often condemned, in a highly civilized state of society.

We hope, then, that in the course of this chapter, we have been enabled to show our readers some reason for our firm persuasion, that there are many circumstances in the past history and present condition of woman which may explain, satisfactorily, the less showy figure she has made in society, without our having recourse to the theory of her radical inferiority to man in mental gifts. But even if our readers retain a contrary opinion on this matter, surely they must be persuaded, that less than justice has been done the feebler sex, in reserving so exclusively for the use of man, the most powerful aids to intellectual culture. If women are of the same common nature as man, rational, responsible, immortal,—surely the incalculable value of such a being is a sufficient reason that full opportunity should be allowed it for the unfolding of all its noble powers, even granting these powers to be somewhat inferior to those of man.

Neither are there wanting more tangible and selfish considerations, pointing to the same end, which may be urged to those for whom this sentiment seems too refined and exalted to be acted upon in every-day life. However we may dispute about the true position of woman being equal or inferior to that of man, there cannot be the shadow of a doubt that she exercises immense influence over him, particularly over his early youth. If, then, we would improve and exalt our race, would it not be advisable to begin at the fountain head? There is surely very little either of sense or prudence in the great solicitude we show about the education of youth, so long as we persist in shutting the gates of instruction against those to whom are unavoidably committed the charge of training infancy and childhood. Will not a narrow-minded and ignorant woman injure the character of all she comes into intimate contact with, children, of course, most of all? Will not children, on the contrary, derive incalculable benefit from the superintendence of a mother whose mind is enlightened and elevated?

We may, therefore, call for justice to woman in this matter, by every motive, from the most generous feelings to those of mere expediency and a prudent attention to the easiest and best method of obtaining judicious training for the young. Accordingly, we firmly trust, that in the course of a few years the most unfavourable of the circumstances we have mentioned will disappear. Since, however, many years must elapse—perhaps even ages—after they have disappeared before their vitiating influence on woman can be quite overcome, we may see how necessary it is to commence speedily, or—if it has already begun—to continue the reform with spirit.

We conclude, then, by observing that there is a considerable amount of public money given in aid of education, both by the general government of the country and by the local governments of the different cities and towns, a very small share of which—in many cases no share at all—is devoted to the instruction of girls; and in many places private enterprise has founded noble institutions for the instruction of boys, to the benefits of which girls have been admitted only in a very few instances. These considerations induce us to believe that our sex is imprudently and unfairly neglected, by the want of any public care to provide good elementary instruction for its youthful members, and higher seminaries for those of more advanced age—or for those who are more keen in the pursuit of knowledge. We think, also, that like most other wrongs, the evil which appears on the face of it is less to be considered than the evil influences which it sheds unthought of and unperceived. There can be little doubt that this carelessness of the public about female education, will produce a similar carelessness with many of their teachers, as to the sort of instruction they bestow; and the extreme privacy with which most schools for girls are conducted, together with the necessary want of any efficient superintendence over a private teacher, afford the most favourable opportunities for the neglect by the teachers of their duty. But even were the instruction which girls receive in private, as good as any which could be provided by the public care—which we think it never can be with the whole sex, however an individual here and there may be favoured—still the very want of that public care is an evil influence which it would be well to avoid. Neglect always implies more or less of contempt; and those who are long neglected frequently begin to consider themselves beneath regard, and sink, accordingly, even in their own estimation—and in reality.

That these are evils which—while they affect in a most disadvantageous manner the whole race—are yet chiefly referable to the neglect of the more special interests of woman by a legislature and by magistrates in whose return she has no interest; and that one of the most immediate consequences of her admission to any share in public affairs, would be, that they would at least be put in a fair way of being remedied, are very powerful reasons for our desiring for woman some share of political power.

CHAPTER XI.

CONCLUDING REMARKS.

Having now, as shortly and simply as possible, gone over the ground we proposed to ourselves at the outset, it only remains to look back and take a general survey of the subject. And in doing this we must acknowledge—which we do willingly, and with the greatest pleasure—that in this country woman is subject to less galling treatment than in many others. She is here allowed so many more privileges, and treated with so much more consideration than in most other nations, that it may look strange if here, at least, she is not satisfied with her lot. But the gratitude we feel on comparing our condition with that of the women of many other lands, need not hinder us attempting to free ourselves from those disadvantages which still cling to our sex even where it is most favoured.

In looking to the progress of woman in our own country, and to the many varying stations she occupies in foreign lands, we perceive that she rises or falls in intelligence, capacity, moral dignity, and real excellence of every kind, just in proportion to the honour or contempt with which she is regarded. Where she is honoured, the nobleness and worth of her nature develop themselves freely, and she becomes really more and more worthy of esteem; where she is contemned, all the finer qualities of her nature are overclouded and extinguished, and she really sinks in the scale of being. Have we not, then, the highest motives for desiring that, in our own country, she should be still more highly honoured—still more freely trusted? In the history of the past we have ample security that a general improvement of character, a higher and higher standard of excellence, would be the gradual consequence of an improvement of outward influences,—and that not only in the direction in which the outward improvement is made, but in the whole circle of duty. The freer scope the mind has to attain full stature and healthy vigour, the more correct will its estimate of duty be, and the more constant its perseverance in its path. Notwithstanding the comparatively happy lot of woman in this country, we think it pretty clear that even here she is harassed by needless trammels—her mind tainted even by positively vicious social influences. If this is the case in any degree, why should we rest contented with the advances we have made, instead of looking earnestly forward to those improvements which are still before us.

In taking a general review of our subject, the idea that strikes us most forcibly is, that the grand objection to our opinions,—that they are calculated to overturn the natural order of things,—proceeds entirely from a want of faith in that very nature which yet has the semblance of being an object of the firmest trust. Nature always supplies adequate means where she points to an end; and we may rest assured that she will never permit any very general or long-continued opposition to her ways. If, then, nature has made so many distinctions between the sexes, and consequently between their spheres of action, as is generally believed, ought it to be credited that the mere removal of one or two human restraints will have the effect of destroying those with which nature herself has surrounded woman? No. If all the restraints of which we complain were removed,—if the mere circumstance of sex were a barrier to no privilege,—if the same qualification admitted to equal rights, whether produced by a man or a woman, we find too many natural obstacles to be overcome, and have too much faith in the provisions of nature to believe that, even at the very outset, the result would be any confusion of the order, much less any disruption of the social and kindly intercourse of society. Those who fear such a result, show, by that very fear, how feeble is their assurance that the sphere to which they would have woman confined is really the only sphere appointed her by Providence. The providence of God has set bounds to the sea; does man, then, find it necessary to give his feeble aid of dikes and ramparts to assist this provision of nature? Or, is it not rather when he drives back the ocean, and takes possession of its bed, that these dikes and ramparts become necessary to restrain the mighty deep? Nay, were every such bulwark of man against the ocean destroyed in an instant, would even the strong reaction against restraint enable it to advance beyond its natural limits? As surely, although woman were as free as the winds, she will never go beyond the sphere appointed her by Providence.

These fears of confusion and disorder in society, were the circumstance of sex alone not allowed to operate as a disqualification for any privilege, appear to take two directions. The first, that it would occasion a hostile collision between the sexes; the other, that the household virtues, and domestic duties and pleasures of woman, would alike be neglected and spurned for what we may call more ambitious pursuits. But are fears, in either of these directions, at all compatible with the idea, much less with a sincere and hearty belief in the idea, that the sexes are marked by nature with many distinctions, both physical and mental, fitting them for different spheres of action which have been appointed by Providence?

A moment's retrospective glance at the progress of civilisation and woman,—for they advance side by side,—will show us how little reason there is to dread any angry collision between the sexes. It is only as civilisation advances that we see physical force begin to lose that absolute sway which it bears in all barbarous or semi-barbarous states. Hitherto, even in our own country, it has not allowed perfectly fair scope to moral and intellectual strength; still, however, we see clearly enough that, in proportion as the power of physical force has declined, and the power of reason and intellect have advanced, the position and influence of woman have advanced and improved also. No remark can be truer than that the influence of woman—where any freedom of social intercourse is allowed between the sexes—is highly favourable to civilisation. She advances refinement and civilisation, and is, in turn, advanced by them. But as this improvement in her condition seems natural to the progress of society,—as it has been brought about by no female partisanship,—and has never been grudged her by man, may we not justly expect in the still farther progress of society, to see her released, with the hearty goodwill and assistance of man himself, from every shackle additional to those which society imposes on man?—from those imposed by nature, of course, no human hand can set her free.

This fear springs chiefly from an assumption—and a most unwarrantable assumption it is—that such views as ours will be advocated by female partisans alone; and that the privileges we seek, if obtained at all, will be so in direct opposition to man. But woman never has obtained, and never will obtain, anything which is directly opposed to man. If this is opposed by man, she will not obtain it; if it is favoured by him, the same sense of right and justice which induced him to support her claims, will hinder him from showing any jealous opposition to the consequences of admitting them. As female partisanship has not hitherto been employed as a means of elevating the sex, we do not fear that it alone will be employed in agitating for these privileges. What we wish, and what alone we are likely to see, is, that the sexes should go hand in hand in their endeavours to better the condition of woman. Did the mass of women hold such opinions as ours before they were acknowledged to be just by the mass of men, then there might be some reasonable fears,—not, indeed, of any collision, but perhaps of some angry feelings between the sexes. But a single glance at society is all that is necessary to assure us that this never can be the case. The mass of women are too timid to think they have a right, much less to make a claim which is likely to be disputed by the mass of men. We believe that the sentiments we have expressed are held by fully as many men as women; and, since the subject might otherwise be productive of some un-easiness between the sexes, we are as well pleased that it is so. Since even, at present, there are many men who acknowledge the justice of our claims, we may fairly hope that that number will steadily increase, till, at some future period, we shall see the laws specially affecting the sex taken into consideration, and their rigour softened. Perhaps even the first readjustment of the representation may see particular classes of women admitted to the franchise, without any disturbance being made about the matter.

Let us trust with confidence in the power of opinion to operate, even on selfish and interested minds, in favour of truth. Do we not see that reason, justice, and the spirit of benevolence, ever make progress,—forcing the most powerful and apparently irradicable prejudices, in time, to yield to their power? If it be really a good and true principle which we have obtained a glimpse of, continued discussion will soften and remove prejudice, bring about conviction, and—as it has already done in many notable instances—convert a small minority into a triumphant majority.

We are equally secure in the provisions of nature from any undue ruffling of the current of society in the other direction towards which the fears of the timid point. And when the truly noble and useful nature of womanly and domestic duties is still better understood, there will be still less danger of any inconvenient or considerable number of women becoming ambitious of pursuits in which they are so little likely to be successful as the higher professions; and it will not be ambition, but necessity—a necessity from which they are not even now exempt—which will induce them to undertake any of the lower. Could we believe that the ambition of women themselves would ever take such a direction as to induce them to aspire to such offices as those of legislators, judges, physicians, have we not the most ample security that the world never will accept them as such? With very few exceptions women are physically unfit for such labour as these offices require, and could not, therefore, compete successfully with man. It will never, then, become common to employ women in them; and, if it is not common, it will be no social evil should a few aspire, and that successfully.'

We believe, then, that in no possible circumstances will power of any kind, but especially political power, be an object of ambition to any such considerable number of women as would be necessary to cause a dangerous or even inconvenient disturbance of the even tenor of society. The utmost effect of their ambition will be to produce an easy, smooth, and gradual improvement of themselves as a class, and of society in general.

If we put out of view the exciting of a spirit of party between the sexes which is feared,—and which we think there is no great reason to fear— there can be little doubt that the acquisition of these privileges would benefit woman as a class; and that not alone by inducing an elevation of general character, but as affording the best security that the special interests of the softer sex will not be entirely overlooked in the struggling and striving for what seem, perhaps, through the bustle of party strife, to be more important interests. Only look how the special interests of woman, as a class, are neglected now; it is at very long intervals, indeed, that any measures are brought forward for ameliorating her condition; and when a measure of this description is proposed, it is with the greatest labour that the necessary attention to it can be obtained from the careless indifference of the legislature. Were there even a few women among the constituents of members of parliament, would it be a work of such immense difficulty to induce them to pay some little attention on the interests of women? We believe that it would not. Although they do not conceive themselves bound to bestow much attention on the affairs of those who cannot, in some pretty direct manner, act on them in return, yet they are not in the habit of openly neglecting and despising the interests of any parties who can influence their future return to parliament. Nor would it be found to be different in the case of woman; class legislation will be an evil in her case as long as it is one in the case of other classes of the human family.

The general tone of society will, of course, be improved by an elevation in character and position of one-half of it: and not the least important feature in this reformation will be the infusion into public life of a purer, clearer, less embarrassed reason—of a judgment more disentangled from political prejudices, of eyes seeing through a clearer atmosphere than that of party prepossessions. It is not likely that the perfect apathy with which the great mass of women at present regard public affairs, will ever be exchanged for a very brisk or active participation in the party-spirit of politics; but public life would be greatly improved by a mixture among the constituency of a considerable class who would pay little attention to toryism, whigism, or any of the other *isms* by which the violence of party-spirit is denominated. I am aware that an opinion prevails, that women, when they do meddle with politics, are even keener in their partisanship than men; but I consider this to be an erroneous idea. They seem more keen than they really are, by contrast with the usual apathy of the sex. Neither is it, in general, for the success of any political principle that they are keen, but rather for the success of some dear friend. The partisanship hitherto exhibited by woman, has been called political by mistake: it has, I believe, in almost every case been a personal partisanship. And it does not, in my opinion, afford anything like satisfactory evidence for believing that woman will not carry out into their views of public affairs,—when they really form their own opinions on their own responsibility,—that disinterestedness and consideration for others, in which they are generally allowed to excel so much in common life.

If we cannot hope that the greater mixture of the fair and gentle in political intercourse, would quite prevent the excesses of party-spirit, at least we may hope that it would do to public life what it has already done to general society,—refine and purify its tone, and soften that unchristian bitterness of spirit which too often pervades it. Were the attention of woman more directed to this subject, she might be the means of introducing into the minds of public men more earnest thoughts of the importance of their trust, and more willing self-sacrifice in the discharge of duty. She might assist greatly to modify that spirit which makes our rulers so ambitious of personal aggrandizement, converting it into more eager solicitude for the public good.

It is that confusion of ideas which confounds politics with party-spirit, which has given rise to the very common prejudice against women taking any interest in politics. The violence of party-spirit—like every other violence—is certainly very unbecoming in a woman; but if we take politics in the large and high sense in which it stands for patriotism and philanthropy, the assertion, that an interest in it is out of place in the breast of the very gentlest of her sex,—in other words, that it is improper and unbecoming in a woman to take a deep interest in the affairs of her country and of humanity,—is made with more boldness and confidence, than regard to reason and truth. The ancients hardly had the idea of universal benevolence awakened in their minds; patriotism was the utmost to which their benevolence practically extended,—a patriotism too often indulged at the expense of justice and humanity. But such as the patriotism was, what would a Roman or a Grecian woman have thought, had she been told that she ought to have no interest in it?

If we could look to society with reference to the condition of woman, from different points of view, what a curious—what a contradictory spectacle presents itself! On the one side, we see a trembling alarm lest the removal of a few conventional barriers should induce what could only be a very partial desertion of home-duties and pleasures; on the other, we see a most apathetic indifference to that unhealthy state of society which uses so forcible a weapon as the fear of want, to drive away from their acknowledged duties, and from what many think their only legitimate employments, immense numbers of the softer sex. It is not alone among the lower classes, and in the manufacturing districts, that an absolute desertion of her peculiar duties,—an utter abandonment of personal care for the education or training of her children,—and a life devoted to labour,—are necessary to save her—and, indeed, do not always save her—from the harassing effects of poverty and want: evils to which, however, she would be exposed with more deadly certainty, were she to prefer the peculiar duties of her sex to those of humanity.

There are then, even in the present constitution of society, many elements which are much more fatal to the household virtues and domestic duties of woman, than the removal of restraints confining her to these could possibly be. We experience, even now, many contingencies, as well as some confirmed habits of society, which absolutely exert an irresistible force to thrust woman from domestic affairs—a force which would not be exerted by the most perfect freedom. Liberty, at the utmost stretch, would only allow her to leave the domestic sphere if she chose; but, in the other case, we see a strong outward pressure exerted to deny her the power of remaining in that sphere, even should she be so inclined! If we cannot, by any regulations, prevent the necessity which induces so many women to devote themselves to labour for themselves and those who are dear to them,—if we do not even wish to prevent this necessity, but rather, on the contrary, to provide greater facilities for female exertion,—is it fair to keep up the distinctions in the opposite quarter? If the necessities of our social system force one part of the sex to leave the domestic sphere entirely, to work at some trade or business,—surely it is a mere pretence to make the conservation of this peculiar sphere an excuse for hindering some others of the sex from leaving it, in the very slight degree which is necessary to enable them to exercise all the privileges we seek for them. It certainly takes them a thousand times more out of the domestic sphere, to make them work for themselves, than it would be at all likely to do, to allow them a share in the franchise. But there is no great likelihood of any pains being taken to provide against women being obliged to leave their household affairs, on the working side: there is no general opinion that it is a hardship for her to labour. If there is any concern at all on the subject, it takes the more reasonable form of a wish that her choice of occupations was not so very stinted as it is,—a wish in which we largely sympathize.

We have still to add a few words to those of our readers who may approve of women taking an interest in politics, but who may think, at the same time, that female influence is a very good substitute for the more direct and straight-forward course of allowing them to express their opinions by voting. We think, that as a substitute for the open and direct method, female influence is a mere phantasm: either it means nothing at all, else it has a bad meaning. It resolves itself into the same kind of influence as is exerted by clear reason and strong argument, whether produced by a man or a woman—whether spoken or written; or else it is an instrument which no conscientious woman could justify herself in the use of. If a lady, by force of reason alone, brings a gentleman round to her view of any question, it is an abuse of the term, to say that this is accomplished by female influence: it is an influence which might as well have been employed by another man,—by the still colder means of a book even,—or by the more careful consideration of the subject by the gentleman himself. If, however, failing to convince his understanding, she succeeds in subduing it to her will by female arts and blandishments, this would, indeed, be the triumph of female influence, but such a triumph as no honourable woman would ever avail herself of. Thus, we see that the influence of woman is either of the same nature as that which is exerted by men themselves,—and which does not derogate in the slightest from their other privileges,—or else it is of so dishonest and corrupting a nature, that nothing could justify the use of it to a woman of principle.

Since, then, there is no good reason for considering influence in the light of a substitute in this case, on what other footing, save one of equality with man, can the rights of woman rest with security? How vague, how dreamy, how impossible to be defined, are the grounds of her present privileges! Unless, indeed, we rest them on the same foundation as those of the lower animals,—which seems to me to carry the stamp of error on the very face of it.

A PLEA FOR WOMAN

"HE gave us only over beast, fish, fowl,
Dominin absolute ———
——— human left from human free."

We are well aware that some rather extravagant pretensions have been put forth by a few writers of both sexes on behalf of woman; but certainly the idea, that one-half, more or less, of our race are to rest all claims to consideration—all claims to justice—on no other, no higher foundation than that on which the claims of the brutes to kindly treatment rest, wanders, most obviously, as far from truth as any opposite error which may have been fallen into in the endeavour to get quit of it. Those who have thought of woman as capable of disputing with man for the sovereignty of the world, have fallen indeed into error, but not into more gross error than that from which they escaped, and in which so many still linger: they were but darkly groping their way after a truth, towards the full development of which many may yet require to contribute their assistance.

Should we be found, even in a small degree, to have assisted this development, or helped, even slightly, to dispel any of the numberless prejudices and prepossessions which surround the subject, we shall not have bestowed our labour—nor the reader his attention—in vain.

THE END

MORE POLYGON TITLES

THE WOMAN'S BIBLE
The Original Feminist Attack on the Bible
by Elizabeth Cady Stanton
Paper 0 904919 96 X   £5.95

THE OTHER VOICE
Scottish women's writings since 1808
edited by Moira Burgess
Cased 0 948275 39 1   £12.95
Paper 0 948275 31 6   £5.95

ORIGINAL PRINTS Volume II
New writing from Scottish women
Introduction by Elspeth Davie
Paper 0 948275 30 8   £3.95

DREAMING FRANKENSTEIN
& COLLECTED POEMS
by Liz Lochhead
Paper 0 904919 80 3   £4.95

TRUE CONFESSIONS
& NEW CLICHÉS
by Liz Lochhead
Paper 0 904919 90 0   £4.95

MEGGIE'S JOURNEYS
by Margaret D'Ambrosio
Paper 0 948275 44 8   £4.95